Journey into Apartheid

By the same author

The Saga of God Incarnate, *1985*
(*enlarged edition with critical dialogue 1988*)
Loyal to King Billy: a Portrait of the Ulster Protestants, *1987*
Making Sense of Religion, *1989*

JOURNEY INTO APARTHEID

Robert G. Crawford

EPWORTH PRESS

All rights reserved. No part of this publication may be
reproduced, stored in a retrieval system, or transmitted,
in any form or by any means, electronic, mechanical,
photocopying, recording or otherwise, without the prior
permission of the publisher, Epworth Press

© Robert G. Crawford 1989

7162 0457 6

First published 1989
by Epworth Press, Room 190, 1 Central Buildings
Westminster, London SW1

Typeset by Gloucester Typesetting Services
and printed in Great Britain by
Richard Clay Ltd, Bungay

To all those who are striving
for a just and peaceful South Africa

The publishers wish to thank the Revd Dr C. S. Rodd, Editor of the *Expository Times*, for his permission to reprint some material from an article written by the author for that journal.

Contents

	Map of South Africa	ix
	Foreword	xi
One	Arrival	1
Two	The Mother City	18
Three	The Road to the North	42
Four	A State of Emergency	69
Five	A Divided Country	88
Six	The Role of the Church	113
Seven	Violence or Non-Violence?	131
Eight	What of the Future?	147
Appendix	Checklist of Parties and Organizations	165
	Notes	171
	Index	175

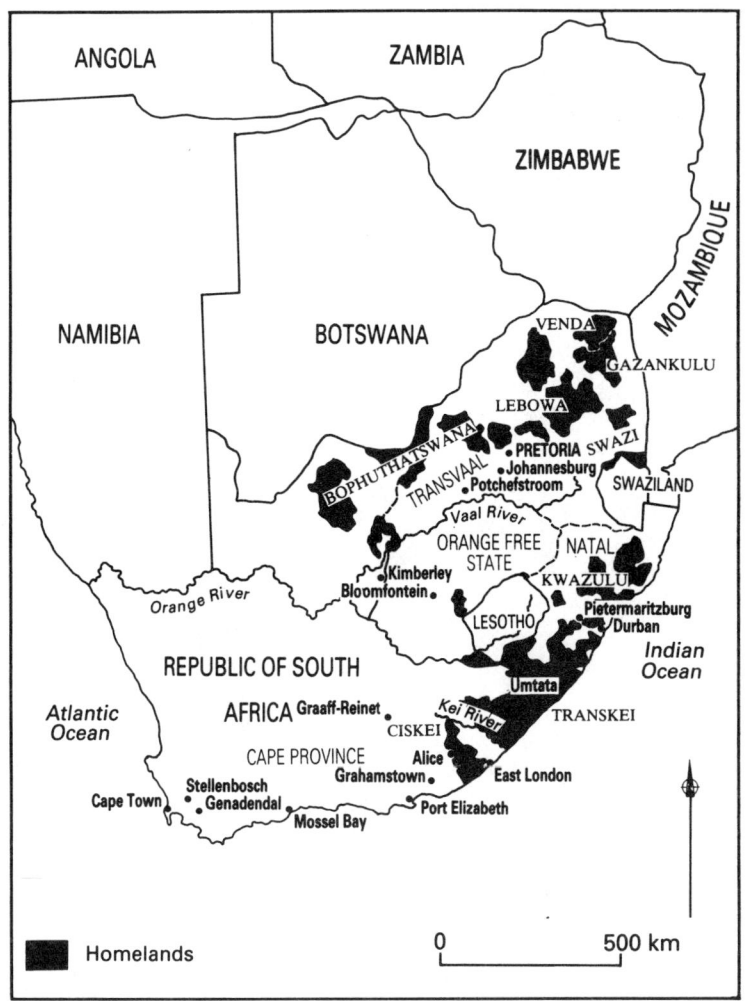

Republic of South Africa (RSA).
A land area which is over five times the size of Britain and nearly equal to the combined size of West Germany, France, Italy, the Netherlands and Belgium. It enjoys a temperate climate and has a total population of 23,385,645 (1985): blacks 15,162,840, coloureds 2,832,705, Indians 821,361 and whites 4,568,739.

Foreword

This book is written from experience of living in South Africa for a number of years and extensive travel throughout the country. The basic aim is to introduce the people and the problems and to show how the current racial conflict has emerged from historical, religious and social roots. But it is also hoped that something of the beauty and magic of the country will be experienced, for, despite its problems, South Africa exercises such a spell that it is difficult to stay away from it. This must be the worst experience of the exile.

It might be argued that only those born in the country and who have lived all their lives there have the right to write a book about it. No doubt there is truth in this argument and a number of books have been written about the struggle by such people – contending for the black or white point of view – but it must be admitted, that few of them have escaped the charge of subjectivity and prejudice. It may be, therefore, that this book, based as it is on firsthand experience but expressing an external perspective, may attain a degree of objectivity which will be useful to those who wish to understand the situation as it is. Certainly, in the light of recent reporting by the media, a redress of the balance is needed if we are to try to understand the complexity of the situation.

As I look back on my experience in the Republic – sometimes happy and sometimes sad – I would like to thank all those people who were willing to discuss the situation with me. This must include not only bishops, politicians, academics and businessmen, but the average citizen both black and white whose views are often overlooked. The friendliness and hospitality exceeded all my hopes and my earnest desire is that the book will contribute something towards the solution of the problems there.

I am also indebted to the Revd John Stacey and the Editorial Board of the Epworth Press for their interest in the manuscript and the helpful suggestions they made towards its final preparation. Finally to those three energetic and capable secretaries Miss Nomfuneko Phoebe Ndemka of Rhodes University, Mrs Lyn Pereira and Mrs Jan Palya of London, my sincere thanks.

1989   ROBERT CRAWFORD

Chapter One

Arrival

As the plane made a perfect landing at Johannesburg, the pilot quipped: 'That's the safest part of your journey over, now for the most dangerous!' This caused amusement among the passengers but it soon led to sober reflection as they remembered that the death rate on the South African roads is one of the highest in the world.

However, we drove into the centre of the 'Gold City' without incident. A quick look around indicated that it still retains something of the boldness and brashness of the rip-roaring days of the 1886 gold rush. Even the names of many of its streets – Claim, Quartz, Nugget – and the mansions built by the mining magnates betray the origin.

I found it difficult to believe that only a hundred years ago this city of skyscrapers, restaurants, cinemas, theatres, churches, night clubs, discos, swimming pools, was under canvas. Its growth has been phenomenal so that it is now the largest city in South Africa and the third largest in Africa.

It reminded me of New York with its square streets, fast cars, and the determination of the population to make the fast rand. On the streets people whose origin is Europe, Africa and the Orient jostle one another. All is a riot of colour, bustle, variety of speech and interest. Perhaps it is this cosmopolitan atmosphere of race, colour, creed, which makes Jo'burg so full of vitality and interest.

The city is six thousand feet above sea-level, which means that the tropical climate is mellowed by the high altitude. The whites in their expensive suburbs (each race lives in its own area) keep cool in their swimming pools: there are here more pools per head than any other city in the world. The homes are beautiful, and can rival anything that can be seen in California or the South of France.

However, I got the feeling – an uneasy feeling which never left me during my time there – that this great city with its expensive homes, art galleries, museums, gold mines, is living under a black shadow which the clear sunlight is unable to disperse.

Perhaps it is the presence of Soweto, the black satellite city on the outskirts of Jo'burg, with its millions of workers tumbling out of trains and buses in the early morning on their daily commuting, that makes the visitor aware how gigantic this shadow is and how little has been done to house, feed, and give them political and civil rights.

Soweto itself, with its population of around two million, has long been regarded as the worst crime area in the country. Murder and rape are commonplace in its unlit streets and it is estimated that an average of four people die here every day. The causes vary from high unemployment and poor living conditions to illegal drinking parlours called 'shebeens'. Since the South African economy is now suffering one of the worst recessions since the thirties, unemployment will undoubtedly increase the crime rate.

Yet these same drinking dens have produced very good literary work. Here Nat Nakasa gathered information for his biting vignettes of life and harassment in Soweto and the eyes of whites were opened to a world of which they knew nothing. That is, until June 1976, when the city with its riots, demonstrations, strikes, leapt into the world headlines.

When I was told the story of this disturbance I found it difficult to believe that it all began with what appeared to be a trifling school protest against the use of Afrikaans in the teaching of High School subjects. This sparked it off but it soon exploded into a demand for better housing, employment and education.

The young black of school age was joined by his elders who rejected the system of apartheid or separate development and contended for a share in the political process. The new situation was that even school children had become aware of their political rights and the injustice of the system.

When I visited the place in the early eighties I asked my guide, who had been involved in the riots, if much had been gained by the blacks: He grinned: 'Electricity, the dropping of the language imposition, and some better housing!'

'But certain other reforms were introduced,' I said.

'Yes,' he agreed, 'Blacks can now purchase their own homes on a ninety-nine year lease basis and millions of rand have been promised by the building societies for mortgages. Further, Soweto was granted an elected council so that the urban black could more and more handle his own affairs.'

'That is good, but most of the better houses that you have shown me appear to be empty'.

He smiled ironically: 'Blacks cannot afford them. You saw the conditions where my father and mother were living. These unsanitary circumstances are common to most housing in this place. The real problem is that the blacks earn much less than either the coloured or the white so that they cannot afford the payments on the better housing.'

In 1976 the name of Steve Biko, the student leader became known to the world at large. I knew my guide had been friendly with him so, as we stood there amid the squalid surroundings and watched the small children playing in the street, I asked him about the mystery of his death.

He paused for a moment, as if recalling the noise and rioting and protest as Biko was dragged away by the police, then he said: 'It was reported that he had not been let out of his cell in Port Elizabeth for three weeks and when he was transferred to a building for interrogation he was clamped to a grille in heavy leg-irons. During the night of the 6th September and the morning of the

7th, he suffered brain injury and while in a semi-coma was driven 750 miles in a Land-Rover where he died.'

'But what was the official explanation?'

'Explanation? There was nothing but lies and evasion. They bungled the defence of their actions to such an extent that some of the statements said that Steve had banged his head accidentally against a wall! What a defence! Almost as bad as the surgeon who said that he could not see injuries on his head because of his colour!'

It was a warm sunny day but I felt a chill feeling of revulsion. He noticed it and with an understanding look said: 'Don't worry, Steve Biko has made us all proud to be black.'

Returning to Jo'burg I had the opportunity of meeting one of the foremost opponents of apartheid: Archbishop Desmond Tutu who was at that time General Secretary of the South African Council of Churches. He is a pleasant little man who wears gold-rimmed glasses and whose hair is now grey. There is a twinkle in his eyes and he radiates good nature. He is a very hardworking man who rose from poverty – he sold sweets as a boy in Jo'burg – to become a Noble prize winner and Archbishop. He recalled that Trevor Huddleston was the first white man to doff his cap to his mother and had visited him when he was ill in hospital.

He has continually contended that the best non-violent way to end apartheid is by economic sanctions and he castigates the Americans in particular for not implementing them sooner. At his enthronment as bishop in February 1985 he declared that apartheid was unchristian, evil and immoral, and threatened punitive measures if it was not dismantled within twelve months. Various attempts have been made to silence him including the confiscation of his passport and an investigation of the South African Council of Churches. The hope of closing the organization, however, was halted by the Eloff commission in 1983 when they reported that while it reflected Tutu's hatred of apartheid it was opposed to the violence of the African National Congress which is the revolutionary movement. In May 1976 Tutu warned the government that violence would erupt in Soweto but this was unheeded. His letter to the then Prime Minister, Mr Vorster, was dismissed as a political ploy which in the event was seen to be a very naive view of the situation.

I started by asking him why, if so many church leaders had spoken against apartheid, churches had been destroyed by the blacks during the Soweto riots. Did this mean that Christianity was being identified more and more with the *status quo*?

'Can we expect anything else?' he replied. 'Christianity preaches a gospel of brotherhood, sharing, family life, learning together, the value of the human person, the breaking down of barriers between the races, liberation . . . but the white man who rules us and says he is a Christian separates himself from us in trains and buses, takes more than three-quarters of the land, makes our men work far away from their families, provides our children with inferior education, offers a lower wage to the black worker than anyone else, makes us live in separate areas outside the cities, and suppresses the truth with bannings and detention.'

'Do you think then that the young black might turn to Communism?'

'Some have already done so and others are beginning to use language blaming the State for using Christianity for its own purpose: to keep the black man in his place. I think that during the Soweto troubles many blacks found help and counsel from their pastors but unless the church supports their protests in the future they will lose faith in it.'

'While you seek to do everything in your power to support such protests you are not in favour of violence?'

'Of course not, and here the SACC disagrees with the World Council of Churches which at times urges the use of force against injustice. Moreover, the granting of money by the WCC to anti-racists organizations has been very embarrassing to us since the government here sees this as supporting terrorists. Now it is illegal to send any funds to the WCC from this country. On the other hand, I must admit that it is becoming increasingly difficult for me to convince my people, especially the younger ones, that non-violent forms of protest will succeed. Can you tell me how I can commend non-violent forms of protest to blacks who point out that the resistance movements in Europe during World War II were lauded to the skies and still are, but, what blacks consider to be similar resistance movements, are denigrated because they are black?'

I agreed that pacifism in general was a difficult position to sustain. Moreover, in such a situation many would argue that the Christian concept of a 'just war' would justify taking up arms against an unjust state.

'Bishop, if many blacks see the state as unjust and they are supported in this by many whites, should the whites, who are called to military service, refuse to do it?'

'This is the difficult question of the conscientious objector. The SACC had defended this right but the state has inflicted heavy fines and imprisonment on those whites who have refused to fight for their country. It raises the cry of lack of patriotism, but surely it is better to endure such criticism than the pangs of one's own conscience?'

'On the question of apartheid itself you do not see any grounds in scripture for the separation of the races?'

'I have considered carefully the arguments, especially those put forward by the Dutch Reformed Church, but I cannot accept them. To my mind the whole tenor of the gospel is to unite not to separate.'

'Would you agree that certain reforms are being carried through in the country by the government at this present time?'

'Yes, but they may be, I fear, too little and too late.'

'Have you a message for white South Africa?'

'Yes, we must not forget that the white man needs liberation too. The Christian black man must show his love for the white man by seeking to evangelize and humanize him. The white man is bedevilled by anxiety and fear and he invests enormous resources to try and gain a fragile security and peace, resources that should have been used more creatively elsewhere. We must liberate him from his fear of the black man and realize that together black and white can create a more just and open society in South Africa.'

I was impressed not only with the reasonable approach of the Bishop to the problems of the country but the practical nature of the South African Council of Churches. Most churches were either full members or observers of the work of SACC and this was a unity of Christians which was quite remarkable.

During my stay with them I gained some insight into the variety of that work. Among other things the SACC supports over seven hundred students by bursaries, develops African music and the competence of church choirs, assists the families of political prisoners and detainees, and guards the rights of the black domestic worker.

In addition, particular attention is paid to the problems of family life, migratory labour, divorce, lack of accommodation, illegitimacy, unemployment and the generation gap. A special feature is an ombudsman office which investigates the entire spectrum of consumer problems especially to ensure that the lower income groups get value for their hard earned money. The yearly budget is a large one – over three million rand – and most of it is spent on the projects and schemes of the organization.[1] Tutu himself impresses as a man not likely to be diverted from his chosen path. Numerous death threats have not moved him and his Christian faith enables him to say: 'You know death is not the worst thing that could happen to a Christian.' In 1984 he received the Nobel prize and in 1986 was elected Archbishop of Cape Town and Metropolitan of the province of South Africa.

Some time later, on the way to Pretoria, I stopped at the high granite Voortrekker monument which has been erected to the adventurous pioneers of South Africa. It commemorates the great trek of the Boers from the Cape colony in the 1830s to what is now known as the Orange Free State, the Transvaal and Natal.

As I looked at it and the marble frieze in the hall which records in pictures the major events of that story I realized that here was the reason why the Afrikaner of today is determined to fight for this country. It had been bought by the blood of his forefathers and all of this reminds him constantly of that price. Here is one of the great dramas of history comparable to the American trek to the West. All the elements and emotions of such a struggle are revealed in the engraved pictures: escape to new frontiers, conflict with the enemy, betrayal and tragedy, bravery, love and hate, fear and trust in God. In the centre of the hall stands the cenotaph in the form of an altar with the inscription: 'We for you South Africa.'

During the summer months, the light from the sun streams through the dome into the monument falling at first on the frieze and then each day moving steadily towards the cenotaph until at twelve noon on the 16 December it falls exactly on the inscription. This is the day to be remembered: the day of the victory of the Voortrekkers over the Zulus.

The story compares with Israel and the flight from Egypt. It was the birth of a nation with a leader like Moses leading them through the wilderness to the Promised Land. The tyranny was the British imperialism of the Cape, the leader was Retief, the obstacles were nature's barriers and the human enmity of the Matabele and Zulu tribes.

One of the saddest tragedies was the treachery of the Zulu king: Dingane. At first he welcomed them and seemed likely to sign a treaty of peace with the party sent to him but then he turned against them with sticks and stones. This method of killing was usually used by the Zulu in the hunting of wild animals, not against men, whom he killed with his spear.

The greatest inspirational engraving on the frieze is that of the women urging the men, defeated and depressed, not to turn back but to go forward with even greater determination. The women when under attack not only loaded the guns but when their men were absent, used them with considerable success. The weapons were so heavy that they were often hurt when they used them.

ARRIVAL

Then there was their trust in God which turned the saga into a crusade. Before the battle of Blood River (16 December 1838) they entered into a solemn vow with God, that if he would give them victory over the Zulus, then they would always keep the day as a holy day and a day of thanksgiving.

Ten thousand Zulus against five hundred trekkers! No wonder they said that this was the doing of the Lord! Did he not stir up quarreling among the Zulus before the battle began? Was his hand not to be seen in causing a mist to cover the terrain on the night before so that the enemy could not make an attack? Did he not guide them in their choice of a good defensive position? The Afrikaner does not take into account the superior weapons that his forefathers had compared with the Zulus but interprets his history in the same supernatural way as Israel or the Mormons or the Moslems.

However that may be, their troubles were not at an end for the old enemy, the British, had occupied Natal and that forced the trekkers to withdraw from the land which they had conquered. The British asserted that they had taken Natal to protect the Zulus from the Boer but ironically they shed more Zulu blood than the Boers had done. But they did concede independence to the Transvaal and the Orange Free State in 1852 and 1854, which showed a more liberal policy. However this did not last long and came to an end with the start of the Boer War in 1899. After the British had successfully defeated the Boers they assumed sovereignty over the whole of the country.

The Afrikaner views the great trek as the cardinal event between the settlement of the white man in 1652 and the working out of the identity of his nation and its apartheid policy, but the blacks see the trek as another example of Western capitalism and colonialism, with the whites conquering the heroic natives, robbing them of their land and treating them throughout as second class citizens.

The memory of the Afrikaner is kept 'green' by this monument and the annual symbolic trek of ox wagons from the Cape to

Blood River. When the memorial was completed on the 16 December 1947 a quarter of a million people were present and they were encouraged to believe that there was a similarity between the current situation and that historic time. A small minority of whites were still facing a hostile black nation and the values that they held dear – separate development, purity of race, national identity – were alien to an external world which preferred uniformity and egality. But it should be said that now many Afrikaners see the need for change and that something must be done to avoid another conflict of much greater proportion than Blood River. These changes which are taking place we will consider in the next chapter.

Certainly the blacks do not like the celebration of such a victory which reminds them of white supremacy in the field of war. Hence there has been the call by progressives on both sides that the day should be celebrated in the spirit of reconciliation and integration rather than division. Otherwise, white nationalism will simply provoke black nationalism.

Of course the white progressives have to deal with their hard liners. Dr A. P. Treurnicht of the Transvaal speaks for the latter when he says that Blood River means that a Christian nation has the right to fight for its survival and its national consciousness and identity need not be taken from it by the accusations of racism. Hence the day must remain exclusively an Afrikaner celebration.

Leaving the monument, I travelled on into the fertile valley where Pretoria, the administrative capital of the country, is built. It was a beautiful day and the jaranda trees had enveloped the city in a haze of mauve. If Johannesburg is occupied with stocks and shares and dividends, Pretoria is more interested in the intellectual and planning aspects of life. One is tempted to imagine that its fine buildings, colourful gardens and tree-lined streets encourage the processes of thought and philosophy rather than monetary gain. Architecturally, industrial buildings and ancient erections are combined, without loss of dignity and planning. This is best seen

ARRIVAL

in Church Square where nothing modern detracts from the Paul Kruger Statue and the Old Raadsaal.

The name of Kruger dominates this city by appearing on streets, buildings, statues, and if we go further into the country, the famous Kruger Park. His house in Pretoria is really a museum today with the preservation of his pipes, razors, shirts, bed, chair; and a bronze of him reveals that he had reached old age somewhat exhausted by what he had put into and taken out of life.

Kruger (1825-1904) was the most outstanding personality in the country in the last half of the nineteenth century. The last president of the old South African Republic (now the Transvaal province), he had taken part in the great trek and was determined at all costs to preserve the identity and independence of his people. Steeped in the Bible – particularly the Old Testament – which he always carried with him, he acted like a Puritan and deplored frivolity and any excess of pleasure but he possessed an ironic wit and gift of satire that made his opponents wary of engaging him in debate. Both his puritanism and wit are illustrated by his reaction when he attended a ball while visiting Paris. On arrival he surveyed the scene and then hastily retreated with the explanation that he must have come too early 'because the ladies were not yet dressed!'[2]

In 1859 the Transvaal was rich with gold and Kruger, while welcoming those that came to work, refused them political rights. Despite protests he refused to compromise on this point for he intended to keep the place for his own people. He was very suspicious of Cecil Rhodes and feared his dream of a united South Africa. These misgivings about Rhodes were confirmed when he learned that Rhodes had planned the invasion of the Transvaal (called the 'Jameson raid' after the name of the British commander) and the rising of the British in Johannesburg. In the event neither was successful and Rhodes had to resign his premiership but the whole affair poisoned the relationship between the British and the Boers and later when the British government demanded a vote for every citizen who had five years residence in the Transvaal the Boers refused. Kruger was convinced that this was the 'thin edge of the wedge' and that the freedom and independence of the Boer was at stake. In his discussions with Sir Alfred Milner, the British High Commissioner for South Africa in 1899, he became very emotional and with tears running down his cheeks, cried: 'It is our country you want.' The Boer war with all its horror ensued. At first the Boers, with world opinion on their side, were successful but in the later stages of the conflict they were defeated by superior generalship. Stubbornly the Boer continued the fight with guerrilla activity and was only eventually subdued by extraordinary exertions on the part of the British. Peace was agreed on 23 March 1902 but the British were castigated by external observers not only for their conduct of the war but their treatment of prisoners in the concentration camps. It was reported that by February 1902 nearly 20,000, many of whom were women and children, had died.

Thus in the stories of the Boer war and the great trek we have some of the roots of the divisions between black and white and the English and Afrikaner. I was standing in Church Square reflecting on all of this and looking at the statue of Paul Kruger attired in the famous top-hat and frock coat. Nearby a large number of blacks were lounging on the grass apparently as oblivious of what the statue represented as their ancestors had been when spectator-like they had watched two groups of whites killing one another in the Boer war. Suddenly there was a terrifying explosion and quiet placid Pretoria was turned into tumult and chaos as people ran confusedly to and fro amid the blaring of police and ambulance sirens. I was swept along in the direction of the blast of the bomb to the Nedbank Square building which houses the headquarters of the South African Air Force. The lower half of the thirteen storey building had been completely shattered and the windows of the shop fronts opposite looked as if a hurricane had hit them.

The car bomb had hurled the engine block over forty yards down the road. The street was littered with strips of twisted metal and blood for at least sixteen people had been killed and one hundred and fifty others had been injured. The bomb had not discriminated between white and black, and later, it was reported that the number killed had risen to seventeen and two hundred and seventeen injured.

The traffic at this time of 4.30 pm was snarled up with the 'rush hour'. As ambulances arrived, threatening in their rush to cause other casualties, people kept screaming the names of their loved ones and rushing forward to the scene, despite the efforts of police to keep them back.

Belfast and Beirut had come to Pretoria with this bomb attack by the African National Congress. I edged nearer, as an important official emerged from a car and stood amid the broken glass and other debris. Newsmen crowded round him – Mr Louis Le Grange, then Minister of Law and Order[3] – as he described the explosion as the biggest and ugliest terrorist incident since anti-government violence began in the country more than twenty years ago. He said that he was sure that it was the work of the ANC which the state had banned as an underground terrorist organization.

The police quickly sealed off the area with barbed wire cordons but it was very late in the evening before the crowd dispersed and peace returned. Later that week in Cape Town, General Magnus Malan, the Defence Minister, said that the explosion had introduced, 'a new style of terrorism into South Africa'. There are, he said, all the signs of a disregard for the safety of civilians as the casualty list showed. The ANC in a statement, however, regretted this but insisted that their aim was a military target. Mr Oliver Tambo, acting President General of the organization, and an exile from the Republic said: 'Don't you think that we have offered the other cheek so many times that there is now no cheek left to offer?'

The ANC was originally a non-violent movement and was founded as the South African Native National Congress in 1912. Its name was changed in 1923 with the objective of ending racial discrimination and obtaining the franchise for the blacks. After the Sharpville massacre when sixty-nine blacks were killed and one hundred and eighty injured, the ANC was officially banned.

The ANC then committed itself to a strategy of limited violence, but in 1964 some of the leaders were arrested and at the Rivonia trial, Nelson Mandela and others were sentenced to life imprisonment. We will have more to say about Mandela in the next chapter but we note that in recent times the attempt has been made to limit the scope of the organization by the agreement signed by South Africa and Angola which prevents the ANC operating from Angola.

The next day I decided to visit one of the foremost educational establishments in the Republic: the University of South Africa, which is the counterpart of the Open University in England. But on the way I could not resist calling at the National Zoological Gardens and the Transvaal Museum. The Gardens house one of the largest zoos in the world and from a cable car it is possible to see some of the three hundred and fifty species of wild animals. And the Transvaal Museum has mammals, birds, reptiles, amphibians, insects, a collection of fossils, and of particular interest: fossils concerning pre-historic ape man.

The University of South Africa (UNISA) is perched, by one of those engineering feats of which the Republic is proud, on the top of a steep hill and from there one has glorious views of Pretoria and the surrounding countryside. At the impressive entrance I was stopped by security guards who examined my bag and checked that I was not carrying any concealed weapons. They too have had their share of bomb damage. During lunch, I discussed the work of the University with a broad-shouldered, middle-aged, Afrikaner who was a member of the administrative staff.

After a discussion of the similarities between UNISA and the Open University we talked about the problems that mature students have in returning to study and how this part-time work fits in with their full-time employment. I was particularly interested in the non-segregation at the university and he confirmed this: 'The university transcends geographical and racial barriers and we have black members of staff and more black students than all of the three black universities.'

Future developments were envisaged, so that by the year 2,000 the institution would be providing education for more than 100,000 students and would require a staff of over 4,000. The theological faculty has eighty members of staff and is, after Toronto, the second largest in the world. I had heard that some of the staff were opposed to the then Dutch Reformed Church support for apartheid and I asked him about this: 'We have addressed an open letter to the church stating that reconciliation between the races is the greatest need in the country and we pointed out that the church must concern itself with political and social problems as well as spiritual.' He opposed all those aspects of apartheid which make headlines in the overseas press: forced removal of blacks, migrant labour which means that blacks have to live apart from their families and have no residence of a permanent nature in their work area, race classification and segregated housing. I was glad to see that this opposition was evident among Afrikaners in the early eighties and realize now that it must have carried considerable weight in the change in both church and state thinking which resulted in the abolishing of some of these laws in 1986.

He was also worried about the lack of money being spent on black education, their insufficient housing, and poor wages. I said: 'The blacks have suffered, I understand, by being left out of the political planning for the new constitution of the country since it includes whites, coloured, Indians, but no blacks.' He agreed and went on to point out that the state regarded the black as a temporary person in the cities and intended that he would return to his 'homeland'. 'The mistake that the state is making,' he said, 'is to continue to regard urban blacks in this way for they have no intention of returning to these homelands to which the government has granted independence. There is little work there and they have been away so long experiencing city life that their thinking and attitudes are different from the rural dwellers.'

I was impressed with his frank criticism of the government and his evident wish that all the people in the country should be involved in the process of negotiating a new order so that there might be equal treatment and opportunities. He also saw the importance of changing attitudes within the DRC, for the Afrikaner regards its teaching as the cornerstone of his beliefs concerning society, and changes here would affect his political thinking.

Since many people are confused about the various branches of the DRC I asked him to explain its composition. He said that about 42% of the whites belonged to the DRC (the Nederduitse Gereformeerde Kerk) which was the religion of the first white colonists who came to the country in 1652. Other small Afrikaans' speaking churches were limited mostly to the Transvaal. Then in 1881 the first Dutch Reformed Mission Church (the Nederduitse Gereformeerde Sendingverk) was established for coloureds (we shall describe these people and their origin in the next chapter) in the Cape Province and about 28% of them belong to this church. However, as the settlers moved northwards contact was made with the blacks and they were included in the missionary programme of the DRC. Their church of over 600,000 blacks worship on a separate basis from the white church but there is a General Synod formed in 1963. There are also about eight congregations for Indians called the Reformed Church in Africa, with seven Indian ministers and a membership of about 2,000.

I thanked him for all this useful information and hoped that it would save me from the confusion about the DRC and its branches reflected in the overseas press. 'It takes time,' he said, 'and I am glad to know that you are going to live and work in the country for the mistakes that are made usually occur when people make a short visit and return home with quick answers to all our problems!'

Returning to my hotel in Pretoria, which was multi-racial, I had the opportunity of conversing with a number of black business men who wanted change in the society but hoped that it would be evolutionary rather than revolutionary since the latter

ARRIVAL

would be very damaging to the economy. I was to meet many more of these prosperous middle-class groups in South Africa and some of the following pages will reflect their views.

But at that time I was really excited about my journey along the Garden route to Cape Town and the chance to meet the coloureds, whites and Indians of that fair city.

Chapter Two

The Mother City

The sun rose with its usual splendour as I started my journey by car from Pretoria to Port Elizabeth and then via the Garden route to Cape Town. Flowers were blooming everywhere as may be expected in a country with ninety species of protea. I liked the king protea and the clivia or bush lily and the leucadendron and the leucospermums reminded me of pin-cushions. Later, I was to learn that this was the popular name for them.

    I crossed the Storms River Bridge, visited the beautiful area called the Wilderness and travelled through the Outernique Pass to the pre-historic Cango Caves. They are a deep subterranean maze of naturally-formed chambers of such intricate design that they are rightly regarded as one of the marvels of nature. After an exploration of the caves I visited an ostrich farm at Oudtshoorn and was fascinated with these magnificent birds. The female can lay about twelve eggs which weigh one kilo! I ventured near one pair to examine the eggs more closely but the male bird soon indicated that closer scrutiny would not be welcome!

    From there I could have chosen to journey through the Hek River Valley, with its vineyard and fruit orchards, and passed Worcester via the Du Toit's Kloof mountain pass to Cape Town, but I decided to stay overnight at Mossel Bay and drive to Swellendam, through the wheat and fruit country, and then get a view of the Cape Peninsula before entering the city. In either case the magnificent coastline which borders the Indian ocean offers a breath-

THE MOTHER CITY

taking variety of lakes, lagoons, forests, beaches and mountains.

In the morning I was awakened by the bright sunlight streaming into the room and the sound of a steam train travelling on a track which divided the grounds of the hotel from the beach: sweet music to the train enthusiasts who come to see and hear from all over the world. Later, in a stroll along the beach, I discovered a train, all bright and shining, drawn up beside the harbour and near it a small plaque, not to commemorate steam trains, but the landing there of Bartholomew Diaz, the Portuguese explorer, in 1488. He had four ships and having rounded the Cape went as far as Calcutta in India before returning to Portugal.

Tearing myself away with reluctance from that peaceful little bay I eventually reached Sir Lowry's Pass and stopped to get the panoramic view. The sweep of the land from the mountain range of Signal Hill to Cape Point looks like a stretched out tongue which is thirty-two miles long and ten miles wide; and within this small compass there are the most beautiful mountains, bays, beaches and vegetation in the world. I was to learn about such beauty in detail during my stay there but also to get to know some of the less beautiful spots such as the Cape Flats.

As I continued my drive into the city I thought about that place and the many coloured people who live on its forty-mile expanse of sand. Their origin lies in the interbreeding between the Hottentots in the eighteenth century and slaves imported from the East and Madagascar. These unions continued later with the whites and indigenous blacks. The majority of these people are working class and are employed as domestic, industrial and farm workers, but more and more of them are taking white-collar jobs so that there is now arising an influential middle-class who have been able to take their place in the new Parliament which we will discuss later. Western in their style of living, with their own university at Bellville in the Cape, there are about 2.4 million of them. A third live in the metropolitan area of Cape Town and many profess the Islamic faith which links them with the Malays who live in their own quarter in the city.

Resettlement by governmental decree causes as much bitterness with them as with the blacks. One example of this was the decision to demolish their lively and colourful community known as District 6. It was so called because the city was originally divided into six districts for election purposes. Poor but very humorous and happy, they become the nucleus of the colourful explosion known as the 'Coon Carnival' at New Year. They were resettled in new housing estates but, apart from human considerations, it was generally agreed that this was not only a loss of bricks and mortar but of a unique community. This happened in 1966 but when I looked at the area in the early eighties very little redevelopment had taken place. So much for bureaucracy.

There is a severe shortage of housing for the coloured: some people have been on the waiting list for fifteen years! The number of them who can buy their own homes is less than 10% and this plus its distance from the city centre has affected their new housing site at Mitchell's Plain. Since they have no other alternative, squatting and overcrowding have become a way of life. A state commission (the Cille) defined overcrowding as more than one family (five people) per unit but the average number of residents per unit in the Cape Flats is seventeen!

I had been daydreaming or thinking too much about the problems of the coloureds when I suddenly became aware that my car was surrounded by a mass of black children waving and laughing. I had somehow got off the main road and strayed into the black townships of Guguletu and Nyanga. Every South African city groups the blacks in areas like these which are some distance from the business centre and means that they have to travel to work. This adds to their grievances when the cost of transport rises sharply.

About 160,000 Africans live here and in the other township of Langa. The housing was slightly better than that which I saw in Nigeria but by Western standards little better than slums. But the worst problem is that the blacks are not granted tenure, for the state defines the Western Cape as a coloured preferential area.

They must eventually return to their homelands. Thus arise the headlines in the newspapers about resettlement, influx control of migratory workers, pass laws, fines, detentions etc. Further, the situation is aggravated by a decision in 1966 to freeze the building of black housing in Cape Town so that there is little accommodation for blacks who have legal entitlement to be there. This forces some of them into squatter camps which are demolished from time to time by the authorities amid protests and demonstrations. But we shall see later that in the reforming process a number of these laws have now been rescinded. I extricated myself from the clutches of the children by a liberal distribution of sweets and promises to return and made my way back to the main road. In spite of the danger of another detour I reflected on the other black township of Langa which sprang into the news at the time of the Sharpville crisis of 1960.

Riots had broken out at Sharpville because the blacks were protesting against the enforced carrying of reference or pass books which are a means of identification and introduced by the authorities to enable them to control the movement of people into the cities. A crowd gathered at the police station and they, fearing for their lives, opened fire killing sixty-nine blacks and wounding others. At Langa, on the same day, lives were lost in similar disturbances and soon afterwards 30,000 blacks marched from the township to the city. Fortunately, the march was turned back without violence, after it had reached the centre.

Again, in 1976, Langa and Guguletu joined the protest of Soweto and there was much violence, plunder and arson. Coloured children and students at the Western Cape joined the blacks with strikes and boycotts. The result was increases in the salaries of their teachers and lecturers and a new Education Act for urban blacks. But the same townships figured in unrest and riots during 1984 and 1985, as we will note in a later chapter.

I was aroused from these sombre thoughts by the sight of the lovely white suburbs and the beauty of the city which contrasted sharply with the poverty of the black townships. Situated on a narrow strip of land between Table Bay and the majestic grandeur of the flat-topped Table Mountain the town was established in 1652 by Jan van Riebeeck who built a fort and provided the Dutch East India Company's ships with fresh meat, vegetables, and water. In the shade of the mountain nestles the university, the famous Groote Schuur hospital (scene of the world's first heart transplant) and the Castle of Good Hope. This castle replaced in 1666 the first mud fort built by Riebeeck.

Having settled in at Rondebosch, a suburb of Cape Town, I ventured into the city by rail. The train was segregated[1] but this was not true of the buses which seemed to manage very well without it! A short journey and then a city full of the old and the new. It is the former, as always, which attracts the tourist. He can browse happily in the old bookshops, or dine in Victorian-like restaurants or visit ancient churches. Adderley Street, the main thoroughfare has them all as it sweeps up from the docks to the Botanical Gardens at the top. The Gardens were the original Company Gardens of Van Riebeeck, where he sowed his vegetables to provide for the visiting ships. So with his garden at the top and his statute at the bottom, the founder of South Africa dominates this busy street.

Around the gardens are the fine buildings of the South African library and museums and I was to spend many hours there, particularly in the library reading, among other things, banned black newspapers. Here also is the art gallery, the House of Parliament, and the Groote Kerk which is the mother church of the DRC. It was built between 1700 and 1705 and refurbished in 1850. Of particular interest is the clock tower (1703) and pulpit carved by Anton Anreith from a single stinkwood trunk. The DRC supported the state's policy of the separate development of the races until recent times (1986) when it confessed its mistake. It puzzles many people how a Christian church could ever believe in separate development and since it was still firmly believed in in the early eighties, and a recent breakaway from the DRC continues in that belief, I mention a conversation that I had about this and other matters at the Groote Kerk. A minister there argued that scripture taught that in view of language, culture and race, it was permissible to adopt a policy of separate development, but I said that such a view, in my opinion, rested upon the Old rather than the New Testament. He did not agree and pointed out that while the New Testament accepted the unity it stressed also the diversity of people and it did not seek to force them into unity. 'But you must recognize,' I said, 'that the current system is doing the opposite; namely forcing them into a disunity!'

'The church must not play politics but only warn against injustice.'

'You would admit that in a country of such material wealth as the Republic apartheid has led to inequality, injustice and lack of brotherhood?'

'Yes, there is a lot of poverty and injustice; but this country is better than other parts of Africa and the black here is now moving into jobs formerly held by whites due to the relaxation of the job reservation regulations. Blacks with education and training are needed in the skilled labour market and as they replace the whites the wage gap between the races will be lessened. The gap will take time to bridge but the way is open'.

'Do you agree with the migrant labour system?'

'No, but you must understand the reasons for it. A labourer temporarily resides in a city or town to sell his labour and must return to his homeland. This enables the state to control the labour force and avoids concentration in one place which leads to unemployment and slum conditions. Further, without this system the homelands would suffer since the people would flock to the cities where there would be insufficient work for them. But having said this it must be admitted that the migrant system leads to the break-up of families, the separation of couples legally married, disruption of family life and no church connection.'

'Does the concept of homelands have its purpose in maintaining white supremacy by excluding blacks from the Republic and thus reducing their number?'

'This argument is often used by people who oppose the plan but what is forgotten is that these homelands were the places in which the blacks originally settled while the whites, coloureds and Asians occupied the rest.'

I remarked that a lot of people would contest this but he reiterated that the blacks had migrated in the tenth and eighteenth centuries to these places (we shall describe a visit to them in the next chapter) so that the state was handing back to them what had been theirs in the beginning. It seems to me, however, that the argument is difficult to sustain and this is the reason that neither the blacks nor the world will accept it. Indeed, as we will see later, Chief Buthelezi of the Zulus has consistently over the years refused homeland status for his territory. However, the DRC has always shown a concern for the blacks and he mentioned some of the many welfare, social and educational projects and the influence his church exercized with the state, particularly with regard to improving the housing provision.

Finally, we discussed the law against mixed marriages and he said that he agreed with it not only on biblical grounds but because on racial, religious, and cultural differences they had little hope of success. This last comment shows how far behind the church was in its thinking and I wonder what he now thinks of the state having decided to abolish this law. Indeed if the church had been more critical of the policies of the government such reforms might have got off the ground much more quickly. This is noted by John de Gruchy in his book, *Bonhoeffer and South Africa* where he deplores the fact that after the killing of blacks at Sharpville in 1960 the DRC had the opportunity of putting into practice the protest and recommendation of the joint churches statement at Cottesloe (1960) but it refused to do so. This statement contained recommendations which were not so very different from the reformist policies of the present South African government, but the DRC did not endorse them. He writes:

It missed an opportunity that might have at that stage in the historical drama led to the gradual but inevitable political enfranchisement of blacks instead of the escalation of the politics of confrontation and the eventual eruption of violent struggle against apartheid.[2]

Emerging from the church, I headed in the direction of the railway station but was delayed by my proneness to bargain-hunt at the colourful and lively open-air market on the grand parade which once was the scene of many a military display. With the ornate city hall built in 1905 forming a background, the market offers everything from quite valuable items to the most worthless junk, but matters are conducted with a relish for bargaining. In particular I was attracted to the colourful Malay flower sellers who offered the most beautiful flowers for a rand per bunch. Gaily dressed, they contrasted with the other Malay women buying at the market stalls who were attired in graceful saris. They live on Signal Hill above the city and originally came to the Cape as political prisoners and slaves but their culture and cooking have now become part of the Cape way of life.

Another interesting sight in Cape Town and other cities is the black newsboy. For him there is no quiet standing at corners of the street, but right in the middle of the traffic waving and shouting his wares. If the motorist does not know what the latest headline is or what newspaper has the best news it is certainly not the fault of these boys who daily risk life and limb to sell it to him.

On the return rail journey I occupied my thoughts with the question: When is the DRC not the DRC? And, of course, the answer was Dr Beyers Naudé. Here is a rebel worth thinking about for a moment. Not only at one time a moderator of the church but a member of the secret broederbond. What could be more Afrikaner than that? But then he got himself involved with the World Council of Churches and he and another DRC theologian were instrumental in forming the Christian Institute. That happened when conscience began to prick after the Sharpville affair. At first it was quite innocent, simply another group debating apartheid and seeking to convince the Afrikaner that there was something wrong with it. But gradually, as it became a more black movement, the Institute concerned itself with the thorny question of conscientious objection to military service. This was too much for a state which needs all the men it can muster to maintain its borders against hostile black governments. Hence for this and other reasons the Institute was banned and the participants dispersed. But Naudé has continued his fight against apartheid with considerable success.[3]

The next day I decided to visit the university and climbed the hill from Rondebosch, past the staff houses, the administration centre, the tennis courts, getting my first view of the playing fields (rugby of course!) which are laid out in front of the main buildings. This setting – part of the estate of Cecil Rhodes, the diamond magnate of Kimberley and Prime Minister of the Cape Colony from 1890 – with its rugged mountain background, is surely one of the most magnificent for a university in the world.

The debt to Rhodes is acknowledged by a statue which depicts him sitting brooding over the city of Cape Town which, below him, stretches away in the distance as far as the eye can see. I wondered as I passed the statue whether his dream of peopling this country and Rhodesia with good British stock (the best in the world, so he said) had had any effect on the thinking which developed the present system.

However, I was agreeably surprised at the good sprinkling of black and coloured students who thronged the campus and soon realized that they had something to protest about when I saw the huge banner which they had draped around one of the buildings. It had the headline: *Remember Sharpville*. Of course these students were there in 1981 because they had been granted a permit; otherwise they would not have been allowed to study at a white university. This followed an Act of Parliament in 1959; but since 1984 the university has been given permission to admit whoever it choses.

To get in requires qualifications, but for the non-white this is by no means an easy task. It is true that between 1978 and 1983 spending on black pupils in schools rose to 146 rand per capita, but then the expenditure on whites was more than 1,000 rand! Since then the rate per capita spent on black education has steadily increased at a much higher rate than for whites but parity is still a long way off. Bursaries and scholarships do exist at UCT but these are limited. Here a great service could be rendered to the non-white students if those business concerns in the Western world which are so vocal in their criticism of apartheid could endow more funds for black education. The fees at UCT are high compared with black universities.

However, many of the complaints and boycotts of schools and universities have arisen as protests about the lower standards of such institutions. In 1982, for example, it was reported that only 4,714 Africans passed matriculation from a population of more than three and a half million.

Is there not a case then for universities such as UCT favouring blacks with poor matriculation results since once admitted they have more incentive to do well than whites? This is likely to be the subject for debate in the future. As for finance, Dr James Moulder, the then special assistant to the Vice-Chancellor, has stressed that no student will be turned away because he or she cannot pay the tuition fee.

However, the growth of black students at white universities in the country will be at the University of Witwatersrand, Johannesburg, where it is estimated that 50% of the student body is likely to be black by the turn of the century. The growth at UCT will be coloured since this is their area.

In the conversation with black and coloured students that I had at UCT, financial and educational problems were uppermost, but I noted in one conversation when the subject was discrimination, that what the student was referring to was not white against black but the discrimination made by black against black! To clear my confusion he explained that the chiefs and other higher-class blacks placed obstacles in the way of him and others in favour of their own sons! Class distinction apparently is not the exclusive monopoly of the Anglo-Saxon white!

In 1981, however, a situation developed which caused much controversy and anger on campus because of the banning of a white student. A description of this will help us to understand what this punishment by the state means. Andrew Boraine spent a year (1977) in the navy and then attended UCT and became Vice-President of the student representative council. In 1980 he was detained for his involvement in the schools boycott. This meant no contact with anyone. Successive detentions followed and then came the banning order which did not expire until 1986. This meant that he could not attend any social gatherings, meetings, seminars or discussions, and might meet only one person at a time. He was confined to the Cape Town area and might not enter any schools, universities, harbours, airports, factories or black areas and could not publish, teach or lecture. This experience of Andrew Boraine has been repeated in many cases and requires great individual strength of will and purpose to endure.

The university was not slow to protest and the Vice-Chancellor issued a statement which was fully backed by the Council:

> What right does South Africa have to be considered among the democracies when student leaders such as Andrew Boraine are banned without any reasons being given and without any recourse to the courts of the land? Students have the right to protest against the wrongs they perceive in society, as do other citizens, provided such protest is within the law. Where it is not within the law the state has more than adequate means to bring them before the courts. The use of banning orders is completely unacceptable and when applied to students and staff at universities, impinges on academic freedom. I protest in the strongest terms against the banning of Andrew Boraine.

Student unrest continued during the early eighties, despite the punishment of Boraine and was symbolized in the burning of the

South African and Republic Festival flags on the day set apart for the commemoration of the Republic.

The staff of the university are generally liberal in their outlook, welcome contact with all races, and engage in protests against the ills of their society. My impression of those that I met was that some were prepared to take action against the *status quo*, others were not, preferring to get on with their teaching and research, and some were very radically opposed to the system.

One of them, who had written a book on the South African situation and the role of the church and whose friendship I was to enjoy during my stay at Cape Town, took me on a drive round the Cape Peninsula. This was such an enjoyable experience that I and my wife and son repeated it many times. It is possible to reach the Cape Point by travelling down the Atlantic side of the Peninsula and returning along the Indian ocean side. I was soon to discover that bathing was much warmer on the Indian side than the Atlantic, though when I dared to try the latter, I found the buffeting of the waves to be an exhilirating experience.

We started from Sea Point, a suburb of Cape Town on the Atlantic coast, with its towering blocks of flats and magnificent swimming pool and then travelled along the curving Marine Drive, past beautiful beaches and secluded bays, to Hout Bay. This is a delightful fishing village which later we were to visit many times. Then a pause along the road to admire those magnificent buttresses jutting out from the mountains and called the Twelve Apostles. Driving along the Chapman's Peak road is actually travelling along the cliff face: an incredible road built between 1915 and 1922, with engineers and equipment sometimes having to reach the sites with the aid of climbing ropes.

Suddenly, baboons appeared and we had to slow our pace; but there was no escaping them! They easily climbed on the roof of the car and peered happily at us through the windows. Then I noticed the unusual sight of a man chasing one. Apparently, he had stopped to have a picnic and the baboon had crept up when he wasn't looking and made off with his sandwiches!

Finally, we came to Cape Point and enjoyed the splendid views. The area around has a nature reserve with many species of indigenous animals, not only baboons but zebra, black wildebeest, and eland. Even on this fine day it was quite windy and I wondered what it would be like when a real storm came up. The Cape of Good Hope terrifies as well as attracts by its marvellous beauty for it is a graveyard of ships caught by hurricanes.

As we returned along the Indian coastline we passed through Simonstown, a naval base from 1741 and now the home of the South African Navy, Fish Hoek Bay and Muizenberg. We became very fond of Muizenberg, for it had a good beach which ran for several miles along the False Bay shore and provided safe bathing and good surfing.

Taking the road inland from Muizenberg we soon reached Constantia, a lush green valley, home of the famous Constantia grapes. Here we paused for tea and then viewed the Groot Constantia Homestead, one of the finest examples of Cape Dutch architecture which was the home of governor Simon van der Stel from 1691 to 1712. Further along we left the car again and entered the Kirstenbosh Gardens which have over 5,000 varieties of flora. Then the return to Cape Town by way of the magnificent De Waal drive. It was night and the city lay stretched out before us with its lights twinkling everywhere. If I had not known of the many and complex problems which it had I would have thought that we were about to enter some romantic fairyland.

On the trip I discussed with my companion some of the proposals that he had put forward in his book about the role of the church in the Republic:

'Your book is likely to be very influential in this matter but you reject any alliance of the church with Marxism.'

'Yes,' he replied, 'though I do indicate why some Latin American theologians argue for such an alliance. Both Christianity and Marxism share a common concern for man's needs in society and both are convinced that the truth has to do with more than ideas, that it leads to transforming the situation.'

'Not by revolution?'

'No, such a way chosen to achieve the end of peace is destructive of the end itself.'

'How then can society be transformed? What can the church do?'

'The church is called to a ministry of suffering love: it must identify itself with the powerless. Jesus always took the side of the powerless, the weak, the poor and the oppressed.'

I suggested that the church had also a ministry to those in power, seeking by such love to transform them. He nodded vigorously in agreement.

'But you would agree,' I said, 'that the state cannot have absolute obedience and that at times of injustice the church may choose civil disobedience?'

'Yes.'

We discussed various forms of disobedience without coming to any final conclusions, but he was sure that only as the church showed solidarity with the blacks in their fight against injustice of every kind would it continue to have any significant influence with them.

This solidarity with the blacks was shown by the Anglican Church. One day when I had spent the morning in the South African Library in Cape Town I walked through Government Avenue between the Houses of Parliament and St George's Cathedral. The latter is a huge Gothic building and had a big hoarding prominently displayed outside. I read:

REPUBLIC DAY (*June*)

No Cause to Celebrate For
— Detention without trial
— Uprooting of two million for resettlement
— Votes are denied to the majority
— Bannings without trial
— Discrimination in all its forms

This crystallized the Anglican defiance. We have noted this already in Desmond Tutu, the first Black Dean of Johannesburg, and now Archbishop of the Cape Province, but there have been others. The then Archbishop, the Revd Bill Burnett, condemned in one of his pastoral letters detention without trial and, at the Anglican Synod in Grahamstown in 1979, he said that they must defy the state even if it meant the end of his denomination as an institutional body. The steps of this cathedral have often witnessed demonstrations and protests by the Anglican clergy, which shows a depth of feeling not usually associated with this somewhat sedate and reserved denomination.

The staff house that we lived in at Rondebosch was very pleasant with a spacious dining/sitting room area and three bedrooms. A jovial black maid came in for a few hours per week and got through an amazing amount of cleaning and washing. She had the same scale of values as the Nigerian maids and stewards preferring to work for an American as first preference, a European as a second choice, and an African last! Apparently it had all to do with the pay, conditions and treatment.

I had some enjoyable conversation with her about her family and her ambitions for her sons. As I got to know her I steered the conversation to the unrest in the country: its causes and possible cure. What surprised me was her firm and vigorous defence of the *status quo*. When I mentioned the demonstrations and protests by the blacks she cried: 'It's a lot of nonsense, the white man is the boss, and that is the way it should be.' I wondered if she was joking, but instead of laughing and smiling when she was talking about her family and neighbours, she displayed an earnestness which was unmistakable.

Afterwards I was left wondering how much her opinion reflected the older generation, especially those who lived in rural areas. They appeared so quiescent compared to the urban blacks. But Edna had lived a long time in one of the black townships. Would her older neighbours agree with her? But, again, perhaps she was just saying that because she was talking to a white man.

I liked her very much. She was lively, humorous, and hard-working.

A problem, however, developed in connection with my next-door neighbour. Not the black lecturer who had just been appointed to UCT and had the most beautiful children, three girls who always wore bright dresses and had bows in their hair, but the Welshman on the other side. He was a very nice man and managed the postal services at UCT. One of his prize possessions was the loveliest ginger cat that I had ever seen and she had the delightful habit of paying us a daily visit. But my nine year old boy had developed a love for a friend's Alsatian dog (when I asked him on our return home whether he would like to go back to South Africa, he said that we must go back to see Rundy, the dog!), and one night she brought Rundy to our house. Unfortunately we were not paying much attention to the dog's activities and somehow he managed to get through a door and disappeared in hot pursuit of the cat. The result was disastrous for we never saw the cat again; and it was months before I could look the Welshman straight in the eye.

The next day I drove along the road to the Cape Flats intending to visit the squatter camp at 'Crossroads', 'look in' at the University of the Western Cape, and give a lecture at Stellenbosch. The squatters were living near the D. F. Malan airport which serves Cape Town and when I saw the camp I got a nasty shock: row upon row of corrugated iron shacks, very hot in the summer and freezing in the winter. Women peeped out of slits in the hovels or clutched their babies tightly as if I had come to take them from them. Men wandered about with that look of despair that settles on the faces of the poor and unemployed. I knew what they were thinking: another government official had come to tell them what section of the housing would be demolished this week. The children came running, under-fed and clad in rags, their up-turned faces looking for something: money, food, sweets . . .

Of course it is understandable that the state should want to remove this squalor, but where are these people to go? Many of them were here illegally: women and children who had followed men who left the homelands to get jobs in the city. At this site or slum there is neither water nor proper sanitary facilities. The state refuses permanent residence here or anywhere to these people for it is argued that if this right were granted there would be a mass inroad of blacks into the Cape. Yet still they come, thousands and thousands of them. This camp stretches for miles and must have about 10,000 people. It is estimated that in Cape Town area there are 250,000 black and coloured squatters.

When the police and workers arrive at these camps to demolish and remove, all hell is let loose as protesters, demonstrators and advocates of human rights, both white and black, try to stop them. On one occasion, a certain Anglican priest called David Russell, having tried every verbal protest possible, threw himself in the path of the bulldozers! Fortunately they stopped in time and he was carried away by the police still protesting. At times like this it is good to know that the humanitarian feeling of the local whites is aroused and they house many of the black families though by so doing they risk prosecution under the Squatters' Act of 1977.[4]

At the coloured University of Western Cape I had hoped to talk to one of the strongest opponents of apartheid, Dr Allan Boesak, the coloured President of the World Council of Reformed Churches and chaplain to the university, about such squatter camps and his views on black consciousness movements, but he was away at that time. A colleague of his, however, showed me how well the university was making progress and what amounts of money (very considerable) the government was willing to pay towards its development; and told me something of what Boesak believed and taught.

His beliefs follow those of liberation theology movements. He says that the black church must become aware of its own identity, for at the moment it is a black church with a white face. This means that it is dependent on an alien theology inherited from Western Christianity which is the creed of accommodation and acquiescence. Such a creed stresses individualistic pietism and has no interest in the realities of this world except to proclaim that the existing order is God-ordained. It indicates that the blacks should accept the position of second-class citizens.

He believes in the Martin Luther King kind of theology which issues a decisive, 'No' to oppression. Since all meaningful black organizations have been banned the black church is the only real opposition left. When the state deviates from the law of God the Christian must obey God, hence he advocates civil disobedience. The only solution to the country's problems as he sees it is the giving of the franchise to all the people. With views like these and accusations against police brutality it is little wonder that since 1984 the police have been investigating his activities and he was detained for a period in 1985. I left, wondering how long he could escape a worse fate.

Taking the main road I eventually arrived in a town called Stellenbosch, which was a striking contrast to all that I heard and seen that morning. Here are delightful farms, wine museums and estates, restored Dutch cottages, a Powder Magazine full of ancient cannon and weapons, churches and fine parsonages, beautiful oak trees, and – in the spring – peach blossom: a town which is a joy to enter and a sadness to leave. If only all could enjoy such living in this beautiful country. But the beauty was created by man: the Dutch made the desert bloom as the rose. They planted the oak trees (acorns from Holland), the vineyards, the gum trees and the firs – all was done under the eagle eye of their governor Simon van der Stel.

Holland is still represented, for as I drove along the road to the building where I was to lecture at the university, I nearly collided with a car driven by a massive man wearing strong horn-rimmed glasses. At the time I thought with satisfaction that if an accident had happened I could have blamed it on his short-sightedness, but later I would have hesitated to take such a step for I learned that this man was a legal expert from the old country itself!

My lecture on current English theology was well received in a vast auditorium crowded with students preparing to enter the ministry of the Dutch Reformed Church. These bright young men asked a lot of questions afterwards, though their interest soon strayed from theology to questions about the British way of life and in particular the royal family. Afrikaans of course is their mother tongue – indeed Stellenbosch townspeople seldom use a word of English – but the students appeared to have a very good command of English so I felt quite at ease with them. As I returned home I thought about those young men shortly to enter the ministry of their church and wondered what contribution they would make to change their country. Would they continue to support the *status quo* or like Naudé spurred on by sights like 'Crossroads' and black and coloured poverty in general, become rebels against the system? It would be a rare breed of prophet who would dare to forecast what kind of country there will be, when they finish their ministry, if change does not take place.

However, change was very much in the air in the early years of the eighties for the state had inaugurated a new constitution for the country and one evening, we were invited to dine with an Indian member of the new President's Council to discuss it. I was delighted to have this opportunity, for the time had long gone when the Indians had been viewed as intruders and aliens and now they were a very influential group in the country. They have a Minister and Department of Indian Affairs (1961), a National Indian Council (1964) and a development of this into the South African Indian Council (1968). It has thirty members, half of whom are elected representatives of communities in the Transvaal, Natal and Cape Province and it advises the state on all matters concerning the Indians.

South Africa's second constitution was implemented on 3 September 1984 and it brought people of colour into the legislative and executive branches of administration for the first time. The planning, however, was done within the apartheid framework and when I first looked at it, I became aware of words like 'groups', 'own affairs' and what is not so closely defined, 'general affairs'. But for the moment let us see if we can understand how the new constitution was intended to work before coming to why my Indian friend decided to participate in it.

There are three Houses in Parliament: the House of Assembly (for whites), the House of Representatives (for coloureds) and the House of Delegates (for Indians). Each race elects its representatives to these Houses and they have legislative power which is also vested in a State President. The Houses have equal status and must be re-elected after five years. Each House has a Ministers' Council which performs an executive role. The State President is elected by a Parliamentary electoral college, consisting of members elected by the three Houses on a proportional basis.

One defect is that the whites remain in complete control, for election to the three Houses is based on a ratio of 4:2:1 for whites, coloureds and Indians respectively based on the size of each population group. Thus the important cabinet in this new Parliament is mainly composed of whites. How different if blacks had been admitted, and this defect immediately sparked off the unrest which we will describe in later chapters of this book.

One other body needs to be mentioned and that is the President's Council which consists of sixty men and women of whom thirty-five are elected by majority vote for the three Houses in the same 4:2:1 ratio. The other twenty-five are appointed by the State President and are considered to have special expertise. Of these twenty-five, ten are nominated proportionally by opposite parties in the various Houses. The Council advises the government on matters of national interest and decides on disagreements referred to it for a ruling; it has no legislative power and fulfils the role of arbitrator.

I asked my Indian friend why he had decided to accept the new constitution: 'It is the only hope left for our youth who want a voice in the political arena.'

'But not for the blacks,' I said. He said that he was sure that this would come and was only delayed by the policy of trying to confine them to their homelands.

'But you and your colleagues who participate in this new

parliament may be regarded as collaborators with the white state.'

'We have to take that chance, and after all there will always be critics of any new development.' He strongly opposed the apartheid system and in particular the Group Areas Act which prevented the races living where they wanted. Often in order to create a white area, black and brown had been uprooted from their homes and made to move elsewhere.

'Do you know,' he said, 'more than 330,000 of our people have been uprooted from their homes over the years. We must put an end to this sort of thing with all its misery.' But he had his reservations about a Western style democracy for the Republic: 'The peculiar circumstances of this country does not make that possible unless we are prepared to accept the domination of minorities by majorities and you are well aware of what has happened to Asians and whites in other parts of Africa when this has been instituted. Democracy has degenerated into dictatorship.'

However that may be, the new constitutional proposals received a baptism of fire from every quarter. They caused a split in the National party with seventeen of their members moving to the right and forming the Conservative party (hard right) which as we shall see was highly successful in the 1987 white elections. The Progressive Federal party (liberals) opposed the plan because the constitution excluded blacks, confirmed white control and gave too much power to the State President.

Despite these difficulties the constitution was endorsed by whites, coloureds and Indians, but the elections for the first coloured and Indian members of parliament were marked by violence and intimidation. The unrest of 1984 and 1985 had its beginnings here. The electoral college of the three races elected P. W. Botha[5] as State President and for the first time people of colour were included in the cabinet: the chairman of the Ministers' Council of the Coloured and the Indian Own Affairs Administration.

Both coloured and Indian communities were lukewarm about

the whole affair as the low polling of 20% and 30% indicated. The blacks were outraged and refused to accept local municipal councils as a substitute for a place in parliament and either forced the councillors to resign or killed them. Their anger, fanned by the new dispensation, rent increases and low wages, exploded in 1984 into strikes, boycotts and violence. The army was called in to restore order and it was decided to give the blacks their own police force in the townships. We will consider the violence of 1984 and 1985 in our next chapter.

My experience of Cape Town was a good one and I had many opportunities of talking to people of all races about the country's problems. The natural beauty of the Cape is a joy to experience and it is sad that people cannot live in peace and justice there.

On my last day in Cape Town I wandered down to the bottom of Adderley Street, past the fountains and the statues of Van Riebeeck and his wife, and looked around the dock area. The docks, begun in 1860, have lost the old pier and the original harbour has been greatly enlarged but the old clock tower can be seen in the Victoria basin. There has been a massive reclamation of land and on a piece of it, looking very handsome, is the excellent Nicol Malan opera house and theatre complex.

I looked across Table Bay at the mountain and saw that it was wearing its famous tablecloth. This white cloud is an unusual phenomenon, for all around the sky can be blue. The meterologist explains that in summer the fierce south-east wind blows – known locally as the 'Cape doctor' because it blows away dust and pollution – and when it encounters the mountain chain it rises and then condenses into a thick white cloud which spills over the level top of the mountain and disappears when it encounters the higher temperature of the air lower down. So much for the scientific explanation but, as H. V. Morton reminds us, the locals know better for they have heard of the legend. According to this tale, a retired pirate – Van Hunks – had a smoking contest with the devil on the slopes of the mountain (hence the name 'devil's peak') which lasted for several days and enveloped the mountain in a cloud of smoke. This contest is repeated from time to time as we can observe!

However, as my eye roved further out to sea I saw the bare featureless island called Robben which no doubt has legends attached to it but for ten years has reminded the world of the grim fact that a famous prisoner is housed there: Nelson Mandela, the outlawed leader of the African National Congress. This island, once a leper colony and penal settlement, had continued to imprison the state's outcasts. Mandela, now well advanced in years, has spent many years in jail for blowing up electricity and water installations and for advocating the overthrow of apartheid. Previously his organization had been non-violent but, growing impatient with the lack of change, it had resorted to violence. During his years of imprisonment he has not been allowed to give an interview but unexpectedly in 1985 Nicolas Bethell a member of the European parliament and vice-chairman of its human rights sub-committee was allowed to see him in Pollsmoor prison where he had been moved.

Bethell reported that Mandela was well, able to work in the garden, study, and showed appreciation of how his guards were treating him. They in turn respected him and admired his courage. Mandela spoke of the armed struggle which had been forced on him and stated that he was not a Communist. In no way would he support the internal policy of the Soviet Union but he did believe in socialism and a classless society.

The condition laid down by the state for his release is that he should give an undertaking to renounce violence but in recent times his close associate, Govan Mbeki was set free without having to do this so there does not appear to be a reason now for keeping him in jail. Perhaps the state is waiting to see if Mbeki, released in 1987, will cause violence or not before risking the giving of freedom to Mandela. His recent illness may hasten that release.[6]

Certainly there are a number of changes taking place in the Republic which would have been unthinkable some years ago, but the reforms are occurring under a state of emergency and the planning indicates a continued apartheid framework. We will show in later chapters that this hinders progress to the negotiating table.

Chapter Three

The Road to the North

It was with regret that we left Cape Town where we had enjoyed so many happy days but we wanted to explore the rest of the country and started off by taking the main road to Johannesburg. It was raining heavily, however, and when it eventually cleared, we decided to turn off before we reached Beaufort West and take the road through the Swartberg mountains to the town of George and then on to Port Elizabeth and Grahamstown.

We really should have stopped at the little hamlet called Prince Albert but, forgetting that the light changes to darkness so quickly in Africa, I drove on and soon found myself trying to follow a winding mountain road with ominous peaks on either side and the headlights making little impression as they tried to pierce the blackness. Needless to say, I received many complaints from my wife huddled at the rear of the camper, but my son sitting up front with me chirped away merrily not realizing the difficulty of the situation.

Eventually, with sighs of relief, we got through the mountains and arrived at a hotel in the little township of De Rust. I asked the man who supplied us with petrol near the hotel if it was a good one and he spoke eloquently in praise of it. It was not until afterwards, when he appeared in the hotel, that I realized that he was the proprietor! Though the hotel was comfortable, the evening meal was cold, and we had to endure his manageress rhapsodizing on the beauty of the mountains. In the morning light we had to admit that they did look beautiful, but despite the lady's insistence that we should remain to explore, we pressed on to George. The town takes its name from a certain George Rex who arrived there at the beginning of the nineteenth century and, it was rumoured, was the son of George III! Whatever doubt may exist about such a story, there is the undoubted Englishness of the architecture of the town itself which ranges from Queen Anne to George III and embraces the neo-Gothic as well. Many of the whites here are English. They have a cathedral and hops grow in the fields.

But it was Port Elizabeth that we found most attractive to visit with its temperate climate, sunny beaches, safe swimming and pleasant hotels. The King Edward hotel, where we stayed, exuded a colonial atmosphere and at any moment I expected to meet an old colonel or civil servant still enjoying the relics of Imperial rule.

In 1820, British men, women and children landed on the shores of Algoa Bay and settled the eastern frontier of what was then Cape Colony. It is amazing to think that at that time there was not even a village where Port Elizabeth now stands. Now it is the third largest port and fifth largest city in the Republic and a major centre of the country's car industry.

As I reflect on these quiet, happy days in this famous port and in the neighbouring towns including Uitenhage, with black and white getting on so well together, I am amazed that in 1985, only a year or two later, there should be so much violence. In the black townships near Uitenhage police in March 1985 opened fire on rioters and it was reported that up to twenty-nine people had died. As unrest continued police with shotguns and gas masks searched buses entering and leaving the townships and tension remained high in the area. It was not only a case of black against white, but black against black, as they stoned, killed, and burned the councillors appointed by the state. This as we have seen in the last chapter, is due to their belief that such officials are collaborators with the government.

The rising cost of living, unemployment, police brutality, and the desire for more political participation, are some of the reasons given for the unrest. The role of the police in such rioting became the subject of an enquiry since charges were brought against them by the Progressive Federal Party which was the official opposition during almost thirty years of government in South Africa; and continued in that role in the White Chamber of the new constitution until it was replaced by the Conservative Party in 1987. Having had various discussions with representatives I believe they are making serious attempts to bring about change in the country, on the basis of peaceful transition. Despite their participation in the new constitution they would prefer a constitution drawn up, negotiated and agreed upon by representatives of all sections of the people. This does not mean majority rule, however. They argue that the plural nature of the population structure means that all should participate in the government by means of proportional representation.

A federal state structure is envisaged by the PFP based on the creation of a number of self-governing states. Each state would have its own powers to deal with such matters as health, social welfare, education, community development etc, whereas the federal government would have jurisdiction over national matters such as finance, foreign affairs, defence etc. The federal and state parliaments would have the right to elect a formal head of state who would be a non-executive President. Since the Party sees these states as small rather than large it would require very careful attention to economic viability, interests of the population of the area and a high degree of homogeneity, in order to make the system work.

But what of 'homelands' or 'states' such as Transkei and Bophuthatswana which have already come into existence? The Party opposes in principle such independence and would favour inviting them to take part in their plan. It opposes their present creation, since by it, black citizens are deprived of their SA citizenship and are unable to make this choice themselves.

The attractiveness of the PFP plan is the suggestion that all representatives of the various groups should meet to discuss, negotiate, and argue it through. And, even more attractive is the suggested Bill of Rights which would grant not only the vote to every citizen but freedom of speech, movement, association with others, inviolability of personal communications, the right to acquire property, to carry on any lawful trade, and to hold public office.

Since the new system of government in the country has not had so far the success that was envisaged and with the continuance of black unrest, it will be interesting to see in the process of reform if some of these proposals are taken up. At least they do envisage black representatives in parliament and it cannot be doubted that their present omission is one of the causes of the unrest. In a later chapter we shall discuss the PFP proposals in connection with the work of one of its most prominent members: Mrs Helen Suzman.

This unrest in 1985 also extended to Grahamstown where there is a large black township but when we saw it on a sunny afternoon it was bathed in tranquility with black and white mingling happily in the main street. It was originally the heart of the 'Settler Country' and established as a military outpost for the protection of the 1820 Settler farming community. The town is called after Colonel John Graham who commanded a dragoon of troops there and used it as a frontier post to repel the attacks of the Bantu which lasted for fifty years. Now it is an academic town and has been nicknamed the 'City of Saints' because of its many churches and church schools. At the top of High Street is the university and near the bottom the Anglican cathedral which was completed in 1828. I was impressed with the unusual entrance to the University of Rhodes: the nineteenth-century old white gateway with sentry boxes on each side and a lamp above the central arch.

In the same street there is a memorial erected in 1953 by the 1820 Settlers Association. The inscription reads: 'To the British Settlers of 1820 to whom South Africa owes so much.' Across the street from this memorial is the oldest building in the city. It was built in 1813 and was a jail until 1824. A plaque on the wall celebrates the settlers with some words from Rudyard Kipling's 'The Song of the Dead':

> In the faith of little children we went on our ways
> Then the wood failed – then the food failed – then
>   the last water dried –
> In the faith of little children we lay down and died
> On the sand-drift – on the Veldt side – in the fern
>   scrub we lay,
> That our sons might follow after by the bones on the way.

Further down there is another memorial, which marks the spot where a tree stood, under which Lieutenant Colonel G. Graham and Captain Stockenstrom decided upon the present site of the city of Grahamstown in June 1812. On the other side of the memorial is a striking portrayal of a white woman surrounded by hostile black warriors. It is entitled: To the pioneer woman and reads: 'Deep their memory green and sweet, they smoothed the thorns with bleeding feet.' It commemorates an incident at the battle of Grahamstown on 22 April 1819.

The Xhosa led by Makhanda (the left-handed) descended upon the city during the absence of the military in 1819. There were about 6,000 warriors employed in the attack and only thirty-three settlers faced them. Victory for the Xhosa seemed certain. Further, what troops the settlers had were running out of gunpowder and no man could be spared at the barracks, which was surrounded by natives, to carry a keg of gunpowder to them. But Elizabeth Salt (wife of Sergeant William Salt of the 38th Regiment) volunteered to carry a keg. This was some distance but the warriors respected women and children and did not realize what she was carrying so they allowed her to pass unmolested. It was quite amazing how she did it, trembling and afraid of the savage warriors who surrounded her, but the Xhosa had never been known to touch a white woman though they often burnt homes and slew the men. It was a costly mistake and led to their ultimate defeat.

Close to the monument and dominating the High Street is the

Cathedral of St Michael and St George. It is built in neo-Early English and has a special pew reserved for the British sovereign or his or her representative. I walked around the cathedral admiring its memorials which tell of the history of Grahamstown as a frontier post and noticed that the bells are the heaviest on the African continent and have a first full ring of eight bells. But I could not help thinking that blacks who enter here must be offended by the word 'kaffir' which appears frequently on the memorial tablets and by the atmosphere of victory over their ancestors. Of course the whole of this historic town breathes that atmosphere and I wondered what changes might take place under majority rule.

Grahamstown is full of churches of every denomination including the commemoration church which was built to celebrate the silver jubilee of the settlement. It seats 1,200 people and holds a unique place in the hearts of the settlers' descendants. It has ten stained glass windows and possesses one of the finest organs in the city. I was asked to speak there, shortly after my arrival, and was told that I should inspect the gallery where the rolls of honour are which record the names of men who were killed in the two great world wars. It was a magnificent record but I also noticed the names of hundreds of boys of a local school who, down through the years, had carved their names in the woodwork of this historic old church!

There was a large group of young soldiers in the congregation when I conducted the worship. How young they looked! The Republic was drawing on all its young men to defend the frontiers and control the problems in the townships. As I looked at them and the memoral tablets I realized with a new force that this country was born in conflict and would continue in that way.

The blacks are reminded everyday of their lives not only that they are conquered people but of the atrocities committed during the frontier wars. It is ironic to think how Colonel John Graham, whose memory as we have seen is revered in Grahamstown, laid the foundation for the 'blessings of British liberty' on the eastern frontier of the Cape Colony. In evicting 20,000 Xhosa from the area around Grahamstown, his men burned homes, destroyed crops, and even killed prisoners. This was done to impress on the minds of 'the savages' a proper degree of terror and respect. Pushing further afield his soldiers captured 30,000 head of Xhosa cattle and left the people destitute and without hope. If the Xhosa remembers its history and the whites of Grahamstown reflect at all upon it then one trembles to think what would happen if the black man had the opportunity and the desire to take revenge.

Grahamstown today is a contrast between the learned and the ignorant. Within walking distance from the High Street is the black township with thousands of people who are uneducated by English standards. But on the other hand the streets of Grahamstown in the afternoon are flooded with schoolchildren who might just have emerged from English public schools. These whites attend St Andrew's College which has many old boys in positions of leadership world-wide and is one of four South African schools which have the right to elect a Rhodes Scholar to Oxford each year; or they attend Kingswood College, the oldest Methodist school in the country and probably the only major private school in South Africa that is fully co-educational. This city is full of good schools for those that have the ability to pay.

Occasionally I saw some black children who were coming from these schools and found it very easy to talk to them. Most of them appeared to be the sons of clergy or people connected with the university or in some other similar position. However, it was reported in the media in 1985 that a large multi-racial school was in progress of being planned for this area and this would go some way to giving black children much better opportunity of education.

Then there is the Albany museum with its attention to the physical characters, manners, and customs of the native tribes of the country, the geology of the area of Grahamstown and other parts of Eastern Cape. In the first year of its existence it had 800 specimens of fossils, and now has splendid premises, open to the public, in Somerset Street.

Of course the biggest seat of learning in the city is Rhodes University (it is quite amazing the number of things in this country called after this man) with its 3,200 students and staff of 1,800. I was delighted to see on this beautiful campus a good sprinkling of black students, as I had noted at Cape Town.

On the surface the relation between white and black student appeared amicable but at times there are flashpoints, such as the university Rag Day. It seems normally to be the usual frolic of fund and festivity which occurs the world over but in 1985 trouble erupted. I noticed as I watched the procession that it was only whites that were taking part and turned with dismay to a black student for the reason. He told me that the blacks were opposed to it because of the expense involved. They thought that the money could be used for a better purpose than such frivolity and when I thought of the poor in the town I heartily agreed with him. In 1985 the blacks invaded the hall where the white students were preparing for the Rag and threatened them with violence and eventually there was physical conflict. Some of the black students were carrying knives so that the situation became ugly and the university police had great trouble in controlling the situation.

Trouble had also ensued in 1985 when a procession composed of both black and white protesting against apartheid was opposed by the police. They asserted that the demonstration was occupying the lawns in front of the main buildings which they should not do because it was council property. In attempting to remove the students by force there was much brutality displayed by the police. Since staff had also taken part there was joint annoyance and protest about this police behaviour.

On a day when it was not too hot I visited the National Monument to the 1820 settlers which is perched on a hill overlooking the city of Grahamstown. It is a splendid complex of buildings which was opened in 1974 and built at a cost of five million rand of which approximately one half was given by the state and the rest raised by public subscription. Standing in a sixty-one hectare nature reserve which is rich in indigenous flora, it has a conference hall, theatre, licensed restaurant, exhibition areas, offices, art gallery, and souvenir counter. I entered the foyer and was amused at the comments in the visitors' book about the building. They came from New Zealand, Norway, Italy, Germany, Austria, Switzerland, France, Jamaica, UK, Belgium and Brazil:

Windhoek – A waste of money
USA – Unusual wind
East London – A wee bit of everything
France – C'est magnifique
Eastern Transvaal – A most confusing, cultural, intellectual experience
Durban – A deluge of culture
No address – God bless you, it's nice and comfortable
USA – Very pleased to see a monument for all
Kenton-on-Sea – Brickwork is fascinating, delicious rats, stimulating pies . . .

Enough said. These were the unusual comments. More frequently it was: impressive, excellent, interesting.

For me, however, it was one of the most fascinating experiences I have had in the Republic. Here is the history of that gallant group of pioneers who journeyed from England and elsewhere to make a home in a strange and difficult land. While visitors may like or dislike the form of this memorial, most would agree that these pioneers demand our admiration and respect. Of course if we are critical of nineteenth-century colonization our judgment will be quite different.

In the grounds near the building is a magnificent statue of the settler, his wife and child, gazing out on the land which they conquered. At the entrance to the building engraven on one of the walls are the words:

> Nor wild Romance nor Pride allured me here
> Duty and Destiny with equal voice
> Constrained my steps; I had no other choice
> Something for Africa to do or say.

And on the other wall:

> We must take root and grow
> Or die where we stand.

Who were these people and why did they come to this land? In the early nineteenth century Britain had a population of 15 million and between 1815 and 1900 exported many overseas. Some 5,000 came to South Africa in 1820 at a time when George III, after going mad, died. It was a time of abundance for the aristocracy but the poor crouched in hovels suffering from unemployment and lack of food. The Prince Regent (Prinny) grew so fat that he figured in a cartoon with the caption: 'If Prinny lets his corsets go, his belly reaches to his knees.'

Post-war depression and rapid industrialization left many of the lower classes in a hopeless plight. Reform of government was to come later in the century under Victoria but before 1820 the only hope for farmers, labourers, artisans, lay in the dream of a better land. This desire coincided with the government wish to establish a settlement in the Eastern Cape, particularly on the Fish River frontier.

What was unrevealed except by some newspapers was that the promised land was not flowing with milk and honey. The farmers, artisans and mechanics, that formed 49% of the immigrants were not told of the murder, plunder, and savagery of wars that awaited them. They were pawns in the British plan for the expansion and holding of the land in South Africa and were required to bolster the defences of the Great Fish River against the raiding Bantu. The government propaganda promised a beautiful and fertile land, a succession of parks, variety of nature, and land (Zuurveld) suited for cultivation and cattle; but a newspaper sounded the warning: 'Emigration to the Cape of Forlorn Hope' and depicted the trials and hardship ahead. The warning went unheeded and thousands of people applied to go but only 5,000 were accepted. I am sure that the unsuccessful applicants congratulated themselves when conditions improved in Britain and they heard of the hardship of the pioneers in a land of relentless sun, hostile natives, and privations of every kind.

As I walked around the building and read about their experiences it amazed me how they survived. Some had never done any farming before and did not know how to milk a cow! Women were called upon, in addition to the usual household tasks and care of the children, to attend to the daily round of the farm while their men were at the wars. There is a description of a group of them trying to kill a sheep. First, they endeavoured to tie it up and having decided to take turns at the killing, they rushed at it one by one stabbing it with a knife, while all the time they were screaming with fright. Children died of snake bite, wild dogs attacked their herds, the wagons suffered repeated onslaughts by Xhosa, and the wheat harvest failed three times in succession. Farmers rode to the frontier wars leaving wives and children barricaded in their homes. Those who had scoffed at the warnings given to them at home soon learned to heed the advice of Colonel Glen Cuyler, the landdrost of Uitenhage: 'Gentlemen, when you go out to plough never leave your guns at home.'

In one corner of the building on an upper floor I saw the agriculture and household implements of these settlers. There was the blacksmith's grindstone and bellows, a butter press, an old wagon wheel, a leopard trap, a wrench, a wire stretcher, a scythe, a winnowing shovel, a carrying yoke, and an aloe cutter. The latter was manufactured by John Wilder of Reading and was used to cut aloe pieces to feed ostriches. A churn was there, made in Chippenham, and a woven wire fence machine manufactured in the USA between 1883 and 1910. These machines were used for constructing wire-netting fences and a few of them can still be seen today in the country.

Portraits on the walls show the part played in this settlement by those leaders involved in politics, religion, commerce, army, administration, medicine and the arts. They were men from the Channel Islands, Glasgow, Cornwall, Nottingham, London, Devonshire, Yorkshire and Kent.

One of the greatest was the poet, Thomas Pringle. He waged a constant war for free debate and discussion and boldly condemned the government censorship at the Cape. By so doing he laid the foundation for press freedom in this country. His poems attracted the attention of Coleridge and he worked as secretary to the anti-slavery society until his death in 1834. I was attracted to a photograph of an original manuscript of his on the old Hottentot herdsman. The original is in the collection of the National English Literature Museum in Grahamstown:

> Mild, melancholy, and sedate, he stands,
> Tending another's flock upon the fields,
> His father's once, where now the white man builds
> His home, and issues forth his proud commands.
> His dark eye flashes not; his listless hands
> Lean on the shepherd's staff; no more he wields
> The Libyan bow – but to the oppressor yields
> Submissively his freedom and his lands.
> Has he no courage? Once he had – but lo!
> Harsh servitude hath worn him to the bone.
> No enterprise! Alas! the brand, the blow,
> Have humbled him to the dust – even hope is gone!
> 'He is a base – HEARTED hound – not worth his food'
> His master cries – 'he has not gratitude.'

I was reminded of these words again and again as I observed many blacks in hotels, restaurants, at the petrol pumps, in the shops . . . The reports of riots and disturbances in the townships did not seem to relate to these people who were so submissive, anxious to please, and well mannered. It seemed the system had convinced them that there was little hope of betterment and that they had resigned themselves to it.

However that may be, the aim of the 1820 Foundation is to enrich the educational and cultural development of all people of South Africa. It also aims to encourage free debate and discussion and to stress the major role of the English language. The latter is well taken care of with festivals of the arts and plays and ballets at the theatre. Conferences on the English Language and meetings of every conceivable organization use the place. The emphasis on English as the supreme communication media in the world is in strong contrast with Afrikaans and I noted that in Grahamstown and Cape Town how seldom I heard the latter language whereas in Pretoria, the Transvaal, and Natal, Afrikaans was heard everywhere.

The major role of English was crystallized in this area by the hanging of the portrait of that supreme master of the language in a prominent place. This oil painting of Shakespeare had been presented by Mrs Irene Burrows of Cape Town. It had been in her family for two hundred years and an inspection by Sothebys declared it to be an original eighteenth-century work. Here there is a Shakespearean society of Southern Africa which assists with the study of Shakespeare in schools, technikons, training colleges and universities and stimulates interest among the general public.

I left the building impressed and uplifted by the memory of these settlers and all the courage and faith that they had shown. Yet I also had a feeling of unease. Some people get the same kind of feeling when they leave a great cathedral. Could this money not have been used for a better memorial? Something that would not attract the tourist and sightseer but might be a better memorial to these gallant people. After all they were poor, struggling to live, sometimes not knowing whether they would see the end of a week or their loved ones again. They would, I feel, have had an immediate affinity with today's struggling poor: the majority of the blacks. Would not a more fitting memorial have been the pouring of these millions of rand into education and housing for these people? When you take the road to East London from this Memorial Centre there are the very poor shacks of the black township. What a contrast between their plight and this magnificent building!

The church that builds great cathedrals and the state that erects great buildings may yet have to face the condemnation of him who apparently did not have much respect for the magnificent Jewish Temple and warned that he did not know people who did not care for the poor. The South African government says that it is Christian and worships in the Dutch Reformed Church. Perhaps there is need for it to heed the warning: 'In as much as ye did it not to one of these the least of my brethren ye did it not to me' (Matt. 25.45).

As I came down from the mountain I was again confronted by a beggar, an experience which is a daily occurrence in Grahamstown. The city has a high number of unemployed who receive very little assistance from the state. The settler I am sure would have cared for him first before he engaged in building glorious monuments to the past.

From Grahamstown we travelled through the pineapple area around East London which is South Africa's only river port. This area marked the frontier in the nineteenth century between the lands farmed by the white pioneers and the territories occupied by the black tribes. It is still known as the 'Border'. The 'red-hot poker' flowers were everywhere and Xhosa farmers tended the pineapple crop. Soon it would be harvested and sent to the port of East London where thousands of tons of shipping are handled.

We headed for the Transkei, passing through the town of King William, en route. I wanted to see this 'Black Homeland' which formed part of the policy of the state to accommodate and meet the need of the blacks for citizenship. Transkei became independent on 26 October 1976, and is one of four such states. The others are Venda (1979), Ciskei (1981) and Bophuthatswana (1977).

Ciskei has suffered severe drought for years and now has vast tracts of land which have degenerated into desert.

When Transkei became independent thousands of people, anxious to escape, poured over the border into Ciskei and many crowded into a place called Thornhill where the pressure of man and beast on the land turned it into a dustbowl. In an interview given in 1984 President Lennox Sebe put blame for this disaster on Pretoria for not providing additional land for this influx of people. Since both states are for the Xhosa people it seems odd that they refused to stay in Transkei in the first place. Ciskei followed Transkei into independence so ironically they found their way of escape barred.

The whole scheme of course is part of the Republic's policy of separate development which was inaugurated in 1913 when the Native Land Act reserved certain areas for black occupation and decreed that blacks could not purchase land elsewhere in South Africa. It was the architect of apartheid, Dr H. F. Verwoerd, who initiated legislation that was intended to lead to the creation of independent bantustans later known as homelands and later still as national states. We have mentioned the four that took independence but there are five more which insist on remaining part of the Republic and another one, Kwandebele, which has opted for independence but the date has to be settled in the future. These states are not recognized by the world and the Prime Minister, P. W. Botha, during his visit to Britain, criticized the United Kingdom and other countries for this failure.

There is usually quite a lot of co-operation between the Republic and these states but one important area which refused to take independence is KwaZulu. The chief minister is Dr M. G. Buthelezi who is quite a charismatic figure in the country and who is criticized from time to time not only by the state but by the African National Congress since he is dedicated to working for change within the system. His land is composed of eleven sections all lying within Natal and it gained self-governing status in February 1977. Having a population of 4,382,000 it is an important factor in the scheme of things in the Republic. We shall see later that Chief Buthelezi is advocating major changes for the future of the country.

Before I went to South Africa I thought mainly in terms of the main racial divisions but while travelling through the homelands and the self-governing territories (there are six of these) I became aware of the great diversity among the blacks. This showed itself in the different languages which they speak: Sotho, Tsonga or Shangaan, Zulu, Swazi, Ndebele, Xhosa, Tswana, Venda. How to achieve unity between such diversity is very difficult and not always appreciated by commentators on the South African scene.

Another question comes to mind: in a majority rule of the country how would these independent states and self-governing territories react? Would they be prepared to give up their rights and join in a united South Africa? Buthelezi would, but on his terms since relations between him and the ANC have been anything but cordial and 1987 in particular saw much racial conflict between his cultural liberation movement (Inkatha) and the United Democratic Front which supports the ANC. Of course the matter is also complicated because opinion is divided over whether Pretoria forced independence upon them or they freely chose it. Another difficult question is: who would support the Zulus against the ANC if conflict ensued?

When we consider the numbers involved in this question we note that in 1985 there were 5,954,425 in the independent states and 6,890,408 in the self-governing making a total of 12,844,833 which is more than 50% of the total black population of the Republic. This is worth recording since attention is often focussed by the media on the activities of the urban black and this big population is forgotten.

Again it is interesting to reflect that if this policy had worked and there had been further creations of independent states it would have reduced very considerably the majority of the blacks in the Republic as over against the other racial groups. This was the logic of Dr Verwoerd! Further, the new constitution continued this framework by excluding blacks who have these homelands to return to when they are no longer needed for work in the cities but it included Indians and coloureds who have no such place. This was one of the reasons that Pretoria put forward for including them in the government but the whites having the majority there could still retain control!

However, the reforms that Botha has made require the rethinking of the whole grand scheme and this has become more urgent in the light of the granting of South African citizenship to millions of blacks in 1986 for such status implies political rights. Those in the independent states have lost this – no wonder Buthelezi refused independence – and the self-governing territories will hesitate more and more in the changing political climate. This too explains the opposition of the right wing of Afrikanerdom and it is contended that Dr Verwoerd must be 'turning in his grave'!

However that may be, life in these homelands is somewhat bleak as we noted in Ciskei and Transkei. Unemployment is high, the average income meagre and some of it dependent upon the migrants working in the Republic, infant morality is high and medical care almost non-existent. Land and people seemed slightly better provided for in Transkei than Ciskei but by Western standards both were very poor. This was conveyed to me not by the lack of livestock or the scarcity of vegetation or the poverty of the huts in which they lived but by the condition of the children. When we stopped they came running, thin and emaciated with dust-laden mucous running down their noses and clad in ragged clothing. Despite all of this they greeted us with smiles and waves of the hand and it was easy to get them together for a photograph.

We were sharing some food and money with them when an unexpected and startling thing happened. A jeep occupied by two black men who looked like police but were not wearing uniform swept into the layby at such speed that it just missed us and the children. They, terrified, immediately scattered with one of the men in hot pursuit. He managed to catch one of them and began to beat him savagely with his stick. I protested vigorously and called upon him to stop but the other man said: 'They were told not to beg and they must take the punishment'. I argued that they were not begging and that I was glad to see them and talk with them but he just called the other man, stepped into the jeep and with a wave of the hand wished me a good trip! I found it quite inconceivable that black would treat black in this way and as we comforted the child with more money I reflected that here was a harsh world that needed a more civilizing influence.

We left the Transkei with a feeling of relief and made for the coast. Passing through reminders of England, Ramsgate and Margate, we spent a few days fishing at a delightful little place with the unusual and beautiful name of Umtentweni. Since I knew nothing about fishing I simply followed the activity and antics of my nine-year-old who found the fish so plentiful and easy to catch that he emerged from the experience thinking that he was an outstanding fisherman! The only difficulty was getting him away from the place.

Then we drove into the 'holiday city' of Durban. A target for the bomb attacks of the ANC, it showed little sign of them with its gleaming hotels, holiday apartments fronting the blue Indian ocean and its crowded golden beaches. It has race courses, golf and yacht clubs, tennis courts and bowling greens, restaurants, night clubs and discotheques, and surfing on the crested waves. The city is full of colour, bustle and gaiety and you can mingle with Indians in saris, Zulus in traditional regalia, Moslems wearing the fez and visit native markets or museums or mosques or Hindu temples.

We were particularly attracted to the colourful rickshaw boys on the beachfront. These boys, descendants of the Zulus who once faced the might of the British Army with great courage and distinction, now trot between the shafts of their rickshaws. They wear on the head an amazing structure of bull's horns and feathers and coloured beads drape their bodies. As our camper slowly passed them, some left their rickshaws and ran beside it, shouting and laughing, and trying to compel us to stop and try their human taxi. But the presence of these Zulus reminded me that we were on the borders of Zululand and that further up the coast was the town of Stanger which was once the great centre for traders and ivory hunters on their way back from Zululand, and further still travelling northwards was the capital: Eshowe.

All around this area are reminders of the warlike nature of the Zulus. At Stanger there is a memorial to Shaka who developed the military training of his tribe and brought fear and submission to the surrounding people by his conquests and cruelty. This region and indeed the whole of Natal once teemed with game animals but the hunter's greed reduced the numbers greatly before conservation measures were introduced. Today there are many game reserves including those for hippos and crocodiles at St Lucia, and at Umfolozi, Hluhluwe and Mkuzi where both the black and white rhino can be seen.

I had hoped to meet Chief Buthelezi but he was away at the time. He is a very controversial figure in South Africa and heads the Inkatha Movement which is the strongest political force among blacks in KwaZulu and Natal. He is criticized by both the United Democratic Front and the ANC which demonstrates how black groups are divided. The UDF say that he gives credibility to apartheid by serving as KwaZulu Chief Minister and by working within the 'homeland' system. Further, they accuse him of trying to provoke the security police to act against them by claiming that they are a front for the ANC. Buthelezi argues that the UDF is a 'slimy stepping stone' for attacks on Inkatha by the banned ANC whose mission – he contends – is power-seeking for itself and it wishes to sacrifice everything to establish its supremacy.

The whites on the other hand have up to now rejected Buthelezi's proposals for power sharing. Despite what the other blacks say about his endorsement of the 'homeland' policy there is in his Commission report a rejection of a separate political future for the Zulu and the advocation of a single political unit out of his area and the neighbouring Natal. Members of this commission whose report occupies seven volumes included members of all races. The plan includes the establishment of a multi-racial executive authority and creation of a multi-racial Legislative Assembly based on universal suffrage but elected by proportional representation with special provisions for guaranteed minority representation and a minority veto. In 1986, further developments regarding this have occurred which we will consider later.

Durban itself hit the headlines in 1984 when anti-apartheid campaigners sought refuge in the British consulate and refused to leave. They represented various protest movements in the Republic such as the United Democratic Front, the Natal Indian Congress and the Release Mandela Committee. They appeared to think that a prolonged stay in the consulate would attract world publicity, which it did, and this would draw attention to their fight against apartheid. They thought that Britain, an opponent of apartheid, would allow them to stay indefinitely.

However, it soon became apparent that this hope would not be fulfilled. Once the Natal Supreme Court ruled that detention orders against them were valid Britain stated that it had done all it could and that it could not countenance their indefinite stay. It was pointed out that their presence in the consulate was disrupting work and in any case no useful purpose was being served by their remaining there.

The move by the British government was deplored by anti-apartheid movements in Britain. Archbishop Trevor Huddleston raised the matter with the UN Secretary-general in New York and said: 'We have had repeated assurances from the Prime Minister that the men at the British consulate should not be required to leave against their will. The only change now is that Mrs Thatcher knows for certain that the three men remaining in the consulate will be arrested and detained if they leave.' Huddleston obviously saw this as a test of the government's attitude towards apartheid and it is significant that he and others thought that when put to the test the British had failed.

The South African government, however, in the face of continued unrest both in 1984 and 1985 detained these and other anti-apartheid demonstrators on the grounds that they were trying to create 'a revolutionary climate which would endanger the maintenance of law and order'.

During our stay in Durban I took the opportunity of talking to Archbishop Denis Hurley who is a strong Catholic opponent of apartheid. I mentioned that I was interested in Chief Buthelezi and his opponents and asked for his opinion of him. 'He is a very strong personality and quite charismatic who, when he speaks in Soweto, can draw larger crowds than almost any other black leader that I know. Further, he has the sense to realize that non-violent resistance to apartheid is the best way. I think he will be one of the foremost leaders in the future of this country as we move towards a multi-racial society.'

'I am interested in the way that the Catholic Church has reacted to the Nationalist government over the years.'

'The Catholic Church was taken by surprise when the National Party came to power in 1948 and began that racial policy which has been disastrous for this country. You know it passed legislation which removed voting rights from persons of mixed race, stopped inter-racial marriage, separated amenities, and even extended this separation to churches and educational institutions. And, it tightened up the laws which prevented the movement of blacks freely in this country. Of course the church thought that the Party would not stay in office but they did.'

'But you have engaged in protest over the years?'

'Yes, since 1950 we have issued many statements deploring state policies.'

'Do you see the problem in this country in terms of racism only or capitalism?'

'Well, they can go hand in hand. The capitalist wants cheap labour of the unskilled type and since the Land of Act 1913 the blacks own very little of this land and have to seek employment in the towns and cities. This suits the capitalist as did the separation between white and black for they cannot get together in order to get better conditions and wages for all workers.'

'I am puzzled by all the various African political parties in this country. Can you explain to me a little about them?'

'Well, you mentioned Gatsha Buthelezi who is leader of the Inkatha movement, whose opposition is collaborative because he has accepted a government created platform as a "homeland" leader. Buthelezi refuses to accept "independence", however, for his homeland. Then there is the African National Congress (ANC) party which began in 1912 whose members originally were ministers of religion, traditional chiefs, lawyers, teachers. Their aim was to bring together black and white and get them into government positions so as to bring about change. Meetings, protests, strikes, boycotts, were used as a strategy and eventually the use of violence was employed. This caused their banning and imprisonment of the leaders. A breakaway from the ANC is the Pan-African Congress (PAC) which is an exclusively African and anti-communist movement. In the 1970s the Black Conscious movement was initiated under Steve Biko which stressed the black man's pride and dignity and its protest was seen in the Soweto rising of 1976. It too has been banned. Then there is the United Democratic Front which tries to unite all anti-apartheid organizations under its wing!'

'It seems to me that the ANC is the major factor today. Would this be, among other reasons: that it is non-racial; has many adherents abroad; stresses class as well as race in the struggle; tries to co-operate with whites in bringing about change; and has black workers as well as students supporting it?'

'Yes. I think too that you need to add what has given ANC international prestige, namely, its signing of the Geneva Convention which involves not harming non-combatant civilians. South Africa has not signed this.'

'But civilians have been killed in ANC attacks.'

'They would argue that this is inevitable but not intentional.'

'I think that the Catholic Church took a good stand when it

opened Catholic schools to all race groups in 1977.'

'Yes, the 1977 "Declaration of Catholic Commitment on Social Justice" is a call to the whole church, the clergy and the laity, to struggle against apartheid. Since then there has been a quickening of promotion of blacks to high positions in the church so that the multi-cultural nature of its witness might be clearly recognized.'

'But would you see a growing number of black Catholics turning from what they call the "white man religion"?'

'Yes, they see Christianity being used over the years in this country as an instrument to colonize, suppress, and alienate the blacks. They are angry people who have stopped thinking in terms of peaceful settlements. In response we must show them that we are in the forefront of demands for justice and eradication of discrimination in all its forms.'

Archbishop Hurley, since this interview, was accused by the state of slandering the South African police by reading a report of atrocities committed against Namibian civilians by a unit called Koevoet (Crowbar). He had really welcomed a trial for it would have made possible for the defence to present a devastating collection of findings concerning murders, assaults, rapes and robberies by the security forces. But charges against him were quickly dropped.

Leaving Durban we approached the Kruger Park with a feeling of excitement and fear. The excitement was generated by the thought of 19,485 kilometres dominated by animals living according to nature's laws and the variety of birdlife. What could be more exciting than to see a pride of lions or a herd of elephants or the slow spiralling of vultures as they circle over a kill? This area would be Africa before man invaded it. But the fear was generated by the thought of our little camper confronting an elephant or a lion at a few yards distance. Would the smell of human flesh not cause the lion to spring or the elephant to toss our vehicle in the air with his mighty trunk?

Exaggerated fears, perhaps, but I did notice that when cars approached the animals, the speed became a crawl and voices were lowered to a whisper. Certainly the sight of these magnificent elephants towering over you in all their majesty does invoke awe if not downright fear! And what of the rhino who can reach fifty kilometres an hour during a charge or the cow hippo who has been known to bite a man in half when he came between her and her calf.

We saw them all from the safety of the car (you are not allowed to get out) and marvelled at the giraffe, the tallest animal in the world, the endless variety of buck, the speed of the impala, the sharpness of the zebra, the cheetah looking lazy and languid after the hunt, the buffalo and wildebeeste, the kudu with its magnificent horns who is capable of jumping an eight-foot fence, and . . .

I noticed that one of the rules of how to behave in the park is that permission is given to get out of the car if a wheel needs changing. This reminded me of the story told by H. V. Morton. A man discovering that he had a flat tyre got out and taking a roll of bedding and the spare wheel laid them on the roadway. He was proceeding to jack up the wheel when someone saw a lioness lying flat in the grass only twelve feet away and shouted a warning. The man sprang towards the door of the car but at the same time so did the lioness – not at him but his bedding! She was more interested in this than in him. Grabbing the roll of bedding she dashed off with it at full speed into the long grass and apparently afterwards had thoroughly enjoyed herself, for the contents were found next morning rent into the smallest ribands!

There are seven entrance gates to this vast park and fourteen comfortable rest camps with most interesting names such as Olifants (its area is excellent for viewing elephants), Skukuza (the nickname for Stevenson-Hamilton 'he who has turned everything upside down' i.e. he made great changes in the park), Lower Sabie on the road from Skukuza and called 'the road of the lions', and the beautiful name: Shingwedzi. The larger camps have restaurants and shops where meat and fish can be bought in addition to tinned foods, curios, etc. All shops and restaurants are licensed to sell spirits, wines and beer. Pretoriuskop has a swimming pool.

The park is so popular that accommodation is fully reserved at peak periods so we were glad that we had booked well in advance. We spent the days looking at the animals and the nights in the thatched roof rondavels under the starry skies, listening to the animal kingdom's eerie night noises.

From the Kruger Park we drove to the town of Pietersburg and then on to the University of the North at Sovenga in the Northern Transvaal. I noticed as we passed through the pleasant town of Pietersburg that there were many well-dressed blacks around who were driving expensive cars. Later, I was to discover that these were either business people or members of the staff of the university which was only thirty kilometres away.

The university started with eighty-seven students in 1960 as a college of the University of South Africa and became independent in 1969. It had its beginnings when the smoke of the Soweto riots darkened the sky and was opposed by press and the general public since it was a segregated university for blacks.

However that may be, it has developed impressively and now has over 2,000 students and six faculties, and has been allowed since 1980 to admit students of other races. Black and white members of staff (academic and administrators) work together as equals. To date upwards of 21.5 million rand has been spent on its development and I thought as I viewed its fine campus and buildings and talked with the enthusiastic staff that this expected 'still born baby' fully deserves the expenditure.

The students who are there now can expect much more than one of the original eighty-seven who wrote: 'Having passed Standard 6 by virtue of my brilliant brain, I now apply for admission to your institution to be trained in bricklaying and lorry-driving!' This must produce amusement among the students as they attend the varied courses in arts, maths and natural science, economics, education, theology and law. The staff proudly point to their visitor's register and the distinguished names: Harold

Macmillan, Field Marshal Lord Montgomery, the Dean of Balliol College, Oxford, Christian Barnard . . . Montgomery's signature is unique! Everybody else has used one line, but his occupies four! One line is open above it, one has the name without initials (Montgomery of Alamein), one for two further letters of identification, and one which has a dashing understroke to round the whole matter off! It stands monumentally apart from the rest of the names, commanding respect, as if, even in writing his signature, Montgomery is taking the salute!

The university is now the largest of the three black universities in the country. The first higher education centre for blacks was at Fort Hare (Alice, Cape) and the other, founded in Natal, is called the University of Zululand.

I talked with a black administrator as he showed me around and asked him if he thought such an experiment had been worthwhile. He replied in the affirmative and went on: 'It was not easy to get acceptance at first. We were called a "bush college" and the older universities expected a failure, but now we are over twenty years old, have a very acceptable academic staff, and have equipped students to take their place in the professions and commerce.' We discussed the curriculum, the salaries of the staff, the attitudes of the students, and the contribution of the state. 'We are experiencing cuts in state aid,' he said, 'as all institutions like this are now, but just look over there.' I followed the direction of his pointing finger and saw workmen and bulldozers busily engaged. 'You see, we have not been stopped with our expansion while other universities have been forced to. This shows I think how impressed the government is with what we are doing here.'

Having gained his confidence and having impressed upon him that I was a visitor to the country, I asked him to tell me what annoyed him most about the situation and government of the country. I fully expected him to say the lack of a vote for the blacks and the demand for a democratic state but to my astonishment he said: 'What I want, and many other middle-class blacks, is the right to be able to live where we want to.' In other words he wanted the removal of the Group Areas Act which for long has been vigorously opposed by opponents of apartheid.

This Group Areas Act which compels the races to live in separate areas has been called the last bastion of apartheid and many feel if it were removed the state's reforms would begin to make sense. Others are convinced that such reforms are merely trying to patch up an evil system which must be eliminated.

As the eighties advanced the blacks led by the ANC mounted a sustained attack on the Pretoria government and organized the youth in the black townships to engage in conflict with the security forces. The basic intention was to make the country ungovernable and force the state to agree to majority rule. This struggle which is the most prolonged in the history of racial conflict in South Africa is described in the next chapter.

Chapter Four

A State of Emergency

The years 1984 and 1985 saw widespread unrest in South Africa with black townships rioting against apartheid in all its forms. The Eastern Cape was, in particular, a violent area with strikes at Port Elizabeth, killings at Langa near Uitenhage and unrest at Cradock, Port Alfred and Grahamstown. Blacks used petrol bombs and sticks but also were equipped with hand grenades and planted mines in various parts of the country. In Durban the conflict between Inkatha and the UDF flared up and twenty-two Indians were killed. A mob attacked a funeral service for the civil rights lawyer, Mrs Victoria Mxenge, who had been killed by four gunmen during the previous week. Homes and shops of Indians were set alight and cars stoned. At funerals black killed black. A particular vicious case happened at Duduza, a township near Johannesburg, where a twenty-five year old black woman was kicked, beaten and burned to death. Black policemen were beaten up and their homes attacked by mobs armed with knives, stones, and petrol bombs.

In the face of all this a state of emergency was declared in 1985. This meant detention without trial, curfew of townships, search without warrant, press censorship, and official news release only. During the first few hours one hundred and thirteen people were arrested but the announcement of the state of emergency was greeted with the cry: 'The Boers are dogs and they will die like dogs.'

Unrest was seen in the trade union movement. During 1984 and 1985 recession and the declining living standards of black workers forced several unions into strike action for higher wages. This happened in the Republic itself but also in the homelands where the relationship with the trade union movement has always been tense. Venda, Transkei and Ciskei do not recognize trade unions and in 1984 Bophuthatswana experienced a strike of workers at an avanadium mine in support of a demand that the mine management recognize the National Union of Mine Workers. This was one of the attempts to try to prevent Bophuthatswana from outlawing all South African unions operating in its area. Since Bophuthatswana is the most industrial of the homelands – it has some important mines – this conflict was seen as most important for the unions.

May day rallies by union members in 1985 protested at the sacking of thousands of black gold miners throughout the Republic. Riot police used teargas and dogs to disperse them as they chanted their freedom songs. One issue was the sacking of 13,000 workers at the world's largest gold mine: the huge Vaal gold mine complex ninety-five miles south of Johannesburg. The reason, according to the owners (the Anglo-American Corporation), was an illegal strike which had been called about wages. About the same time 2,000 miners were sacked at the Hartebeesfontein mine amid scenes of violence. These dismissals and strikes added to the worries of the government as unrest continued in the black townships.

A development in the trade unions occurred towards the end of 1985. This was the formation of the largest trade union federation in the history of the Republic: The Congress of South African Trade Unions (COSATU). It has thirty-four affiliates with a combined membership of half a million; and has political as well as economic demands which are similar to both the UDF and ANC. It gave the state six months to scrap the pass laws which were being gradually reformed by Pretoria and intends to call a general strike if the threat to repatriate foreign workers is ever carried out.

Together with demonstrations, protests, stoning and killing, the blacks found another effective strategy: the boycotting of white shops. This hurt the white businessman but it led to violence between black and black as the militants punished those who refused to stop buying in such shops.

Inspiration was created by the activity of the Mandelas during this period. Rumour and speculation spread that Nelson Mandela, who had been transferred to hospital owing to an illness, might be released; and his wife Winnie, defying a banning order which stated that she must not reside in Soweto stirred up enthusiastic crowds with her fiery speeches which included the vow that 'the blood of our heroes would be revenged'.

At a funeral in Cradock Marxist influence showed as 35,000 mourners yelled their approval when two massive red banners were raised at the graveside: the flag of the Soviet Union and the banner of the banned South African Communist Party. These funerals became commonplace as the numbers of the dead rose. It was estimated that since September 1984 to the declaration of the state of emergency in July 1985 over 480 people had been killed. Whites too were not escaping as families were killed on the borders of neighbouring countries by land mines.

Security became a top priority and the state added four new helicopters and water cannon vehicles to strengthen its defence forces. Soldiers were used to assist police and horses were employed. The police were accused of brutality in many cases since at times instead of trying to keep the peace they engaged in punitive measures.

Reports were recorded of deaths in detention. The UDF stated that fifty-seven of the seventy detained in 1984 had died but this was not confirmed by organizations which monitor such detentions. Leading members of the UDF were confined in prison among whom was Mrs Albertina Sisulu, a president of the organization. The police alleged that the UDF was a front for the ANC and watched its activities very carefully since it had under its wing 600 affiliated movements.

The ANC, for its part, apart from intimidation of the blacks to carry on with strikes and boycotts, renewed its guerrilla war. At the first executive gathering of the ANC since 1969 which was held in Zambia on 16 June 1985, Mr Tambo promised to intensify the struggle at any cost. In addition this movement gained worldwide publicity with the visit of Tambo to Europe, and though he was not received by the Conservative government in Britain he was welcomed by the Labour Party with open arms.

Many reasons for the unrest were put forward. The blacks, as we have noted, did not like the new constitution, but other causes can be detected such as the rising cost of living, unemployment, demands for more participation in government, police harassment, and the hatred of the black local councillors appointed by the state. But there can be little doubt that the unrest was a basic protest against the whole apparatus of apartheid.

The London *Sunday Times* demonstrated the failure of apartheid in a poll carried out by Markinor, the Gallup Affiliate in South Africa, and reported on September 1985. It was taken during August after President P. W. Botha's disappointing speech of 15 August. Of the 500 whites interviewed only 36% said that they were happy about apartheid and 63% of them expected that it would cease to exist. A majority of whites said that they would accept a multi-racial government with 51% of those polled saying that they thought a joint government of blacks and whites would be possible. But Botha remained the choice of whites to rule the country whereas his right-wing opponent Andries Treurnicht had only 5% of the whites for him. However, not one white stated a support for Nelson Mandela as President yet he was the clear favourite among blacks in a previous *Sunday Times* poll.

With regard to change, the blacks showed their divisions. During the visit of Senator Edward Kennedy whose tour resembled, in personnel and methodology, the kind of circus associated with American electioneering, there were demonstrations and opposition from the Azanian People's Organization, who want black power. Their method is revolutionary socialism and they attacked the imperialism and capitalism which they considered Kennedy represented.

This demonstrated their difference with the United Democratic Front which is non-racial whereas the Azanian People's Organization or Azapo represents the Black Consciousness movement. It excludes whites and looks for the rewakening of black pride and self-respect which has been damaged by apartheid. But the destroying of apartheid is only the first step on the road to the downfall of capitalism and the bringing in of socialism. Further, it is divided into right and left wings. The right totally excludes the whites but the left may not, as long as they fight for a socialistic state. The movement is strongest in the Transvaal and particularly active in Durban. Again, it could be argued that there are divisions within the UDF, on the basis that some sympathize with Black Consciousness and were displeased with its invitation to Kennedy.

Of course Azapo and the ANC are banned and it may be, as some commentators think, that it is the UDF which is the most successful coalition of black and non-racial opposition groups. Certainly the state has recognized the need to act against it and in 1985 sixteen of the most prominent members were arrested on charges of treason and placed on trial. The UDF in response insisted that it has always stood for peaceful change in the country and is not a subversive or violent organization.

Again, there is general division among the blacks between those who want to work with the state for change and those who call them 'collaborators' and use violence against them. One example was the Revd Sam Buti who had campaigned against apartheid and for the release of Nelson Mandela but had his home burned to the ground. His mistake according to those who did it was to serve his town as mayor. The more moderate opinion is represented by churchmen like Archbishop Desmond Tutu who calls for sanctions even though they might be devastating for the blacks. He argues that such suffering would be worthwhile if it would bring the whites to their senses. On the other hand Chief

Buthelezi opposes this viewpoint, arguing that the blacks would suffer much more than the whites.

Tutu, as is well known, opposes violence. In an impassioned speech delivered in July 1985 to thousands of blacks gathered for a funeral he reminded them that the television worldwide had shown them killing and burning a woman suspected of collaborating with the state. 'When they see this,' he cried, 'they will say maybe they are not yet ready for freedom.' Further, he warned, that if the killing did not stop he and his family would have to leave the country they loved.

This was a most courageous speech, as was the offer to act in a reconciling role with the government. Courageous, because it might alienate him from many of the blacks, and reconciling in that he said it was not too late for black and white to work out a solution for the country. The state, however, fears that if such lack of law and order was allowed to continue and the blacks did come to power moderates such as Tutu would be swept away.

In December 1985 Tutu again rejected violence and those who advocated financial support for it. He said that certain demands must be met if peace was to come again to the Republic. All blacks must be recognized as South African citizens, apartheid dismantled, political prisoners freed, exiles permitted to return, and negotiations started with representatives of the people. He warned that if the state continued to delay these reforms moderates like himself would 'lose face' as the impatience of the blacks increased.

Another churchman of prominence is Dr Allan Boesak whom we have already mentioned in a previous chapter. He makes no secret of his support for the UDF and was instrumental in apartheid being declared a heresy at the World Alliance of Reformed Churches meeting in Canada in 1982. Boesak supports black theology which we shall discuss later and looks to the methods of Gandhi and Martin Luther King for inspiration in the struggle in South Africa. He is committed to non-violence but realizes that such a stand is hard to defend in the light of the violence by the state. He thinks that the way forward is for the state to respond to the challenge of the UDF to create a climate in which a national convention can take place to work out a solution to the problems.

Boesak has not only had to surmount detention but a campaign to smear his name. With regard to the first he tried to organize a march on Pollsmoor prison in Cape Town where Nelson Mandela was imprisoned but he was arrested and imprisoned. Later, after much unrest in the coloured townships of the Cape he was released and the charges dropped. Concerning the second moral charge it was alleged that he was having an adulterous affair with a white woman. Boesak admitted to a 'special relationship' with the woman and his church authorities suspended him briefly from preaching, teaching and administering the sacraments. But after an enquiry the smear was rejected and Boesak was reinstated.

With regard to change the whites are divided. One of the right wing leaders, Dr Andries Treurnicht, has rejected the new constitution and accuses Botha of having broken up the unity of Afrikanerdom. He was for twenty years a minister of the Dutch Reformed Church and he does not believe that the blacks can ever be part of the South African way of life. He insists that Botha wants to give the blacks everything except the vote.

Continuing unrest has produced a strong reaction among this right wing. Many of them have fully equipped themselves with guns, and advocate a retreat to the laager (the circle of ox-wagons within which the Voortrekkers protected themselves from their enemies). Gripped by the fear that they will lose their jobs and the country if Botha's reforms continue and with the knowledge that they have nowhere else in the world to go to they are prepared to fight to the last man. They hope that they might reconstitute the old Boer republics of the Transvaal and the Orange Free State as their white homelands. Like the Ulster Protestant they gain inspiration from the past and Calvinistic religion. Various groups and parties have sprung up such as the Herstigte Nasionale (Purified National Party) who stress 'no surrender' and dwell on the wrongs that their forefathers suffered at the hands of the British in the concentration camps and the wars with the blacks. They hold that the blacks are a simple people and not ready for a multi-racial society. The Afrikaner Volkswag has been set up which says that the new constitution is the first step on the way to a 'sell out' and is recruiting people from all over the country. Together with the HNP, the conservative party and the Afrikaner resistance movement they provide a formidable threat to the policy of Botha who found himself engaged in a delicate balancing act between their demands and the pressure of the blacks. The right wing has gone as far as forming a private army called the Brandwag which could trigger off trouble at any moment in an already volatile situation.

I was often asked on my return to the UK about the press and how it was affecting change in South Africa and this question deserves a mention here. There are many newspapers in the country both national and regional and at least forty-two are published specifically for racial groups and over the years some have been banned. But it is possible to read banned black newspapers reporting on past events in central libraries like Cape Town, and there is the possibility of appealing to the courts regarding censorship. When there was no state of emergency this appeal was often upheld, as in the case of Mr Tyson, the editor of the *Johannesburg Star*, who was acquitted in the courts of a charge by the state of illegally quoting Mr Oliver Tambo of the ANC in February 1984. The press has often acted courageously in critizing the government and it is a pity that it suffers at times from lack of sympathy from the outside world. This can be illustrated by a decision of the international Olympic committee to deny all facilities to South African journalists and broadcasters at the Los Angeles games in 1984. This was a harsh decision not only because it failed to realize how many South African newspapers openly criticize their government but also was illogical in allowing representatives of the media from dictatorships around the world to sit freely in the press box.

In general Afrikaans newspapers support the state while English-speaking ones freely criticize and have done good work in trying to bring apartheid to an end. One of the best known and most widely circulated newspapers, the *Rand Daily Mail*, which had a large black readership and monitored the government's policies critically, has been discontinued apparently because of financial difficulties.

Under the state of emergency press freedom became very limited and harsh censorship prevailed. Indeed in 1986 journalists present at scenes of unrest were instructed to remove themselves immediately. Various appeals have been made to the courts and some have been successful, though the state is adept at redrafting regulations which have been invalidated.

Another factor that needs consideration is the changing relation of South Africa with its close neighbours and the external world. With the Front Line States, as they have been called, the Republic has always had a somewhat shaky relationship, namely, Namibia, Angola, Mozambique, Lesotho, Botswana, Zambia, and since independence, Zimbabwe. In 1984 South Africa launched an offensive against Angola to wipe out the bases of the South West Africa People's Organization (SWAPO) which was fighting for the independence of Namibia. South African forces withdrew after a month-long campaign saying that they had prevented 1,000 guerrillas of SWAPO from launching their annual offensive into the territory of Namibia during the rainy season. Since then relations have been anything but cordial. Meetings between the two sides rang with accusations. The Lusaka agreement between the two countries provided for a South African troop withdrawal from Angola to be followed by Pretoria ceding independence to Namibia under UN resolution 435 of 1978, and accepting that a SWAPO government could become a reality in Windhoek. In turn, Angola and Cuba promised a Cuban withdrawal once 435 was implemented. Violations of the Lusaka agreement continued and Angola suffered terrible destruction both from the South African forces and two black guerrilla movements, Unita and FNLA. It is generally accepted that the latter are backed by the US, Portugal, Morocco, and Zaire. South Africa has supplied leadership and training.

The presence of the Cubans in Angola confirms the Republic's verbal warnings of the danger for the West of communistic involvement in Southern Africa and then meant the support of the Reagan Administration, though the capture of a South African strike force near the Angola/Namibia oil refinery in 1985 soured this relation with the US. Angola has proved a problem for Pretoria since it is not dependent on either military or economic aid and is Africa's second ranking oil producer.

SWAPO in Namibia has been opposing the Republic rule since 1944, but when the ceasefire between Angola and South Africa came into force in February 1984 the Angolans agreed to prevent SWAPO guerrillas from launching their attacks from the southern part of their country into Namibia. The loss of this strategic base was a big blow to SWAPO. It tried to infiltrate Namibia and became active in trying to convince white Namibians that their future will be secure under independence. In May 1984 Mr Sam Nujoma, the SWAPO leader, said that in spite of bitter memories SWAPO would forgive and strive for a democratic society that would protect the liberty of all. South Africa engaged in talks with SWAPO in 1984 and in 1986 declared that if the Cubans left Angola they would withdraw from Namibia. Nothing happened then but in February 1988 Cuban and Angolan officials announced their acceptance of a plan to remove all Cuban troops from Angola, and this was followed by a cease-fire and the withdrawal of South Africa from Namibia in 1989.

Mozambique has been torn apart by the conflict between the national resistance movement (MNR), who are guerrilla fighters originally set up by the Rhodesian army to counter Mugabe's forces, and the government of Maputo. South Africa supported the rebels but became embarrassed by reports that they had engaged in mass killings of civilians, forced labour and starvation. Thus in March 1984 it signed the Nkomati treaty to stop supporting the rebels on the condition that Mozambique would inhibit the ANC from using its country to launch attacks against the Republic. The enforcing of the treaty, however, did not go smoothly and President Chissano withdrew Mozambican participation in the joint security commission which had been set up in 1986 because he accused Pretoria of continued collusion with the MNR. The whole affair provided a setback for the ANC despite their denials. They had in Maputo a listening post and a planning centre which was less than three hundred miles from the industrial centre of the Transvaal. Moreover refugees from Soweto and other parts of the Republic had, as part of their number, young men willing to join the ANC and they passed through Mozambique to Angola for military training. From Maputo they returned to the Republic as saboteurs but this was stopped by the Nkomati accord and led to a reduction of ANC personnel in the country to about ten people. In May 1987, however, Mozambique accused South African commandos of attacking four different targets in its country and continued to assert that the Republic had been involved in the air crash of their President, Samora Machel, though a board of enquiry stated that it had happened due to negligence on the part of the Russian air crew. Discussions of grievances which are held from time to time between the two countries have so far failed to ease the tensions, but in 1988 the joint security commission was reactivated and a meeting between President Chissano and Botha could take place in the future. Mozambique of course is important to the Front Line States especially Zimbabwe which is intent on developing and guarding the Beira corridor, its most viable alternative trade route to the sea. If such a link could be protected it would reduce the reliance of the States on the Republic but MNR rebels are doing their best to sabotage it.

South Africa is suspicious too of Lesotho and Botswana as places that not only harbour ANC terrorists but are seedbeds of Communism. Pretoria was enraged at the invitation of Lesotho to five Communist countries to establish embassies in their capital city. After explosions in Pretoria and Bloemfontein, strict control was imposed on traffic between Lesotho and the Republic in 1985 and this economic blockade of a country dependent upon South

Africa led to the *coup d'etat* which toppled the government there. Botswana has experienced a number of devastating raids by the South African strike force and these have been condemned by the USA. Botha, however, defended such actions in parliament and said that if circles in the US thought that he would sit back and do nothing while ANC guerrillas crossed the borders from Botswana and elsewhere they were gravely mistaken.

Botha, despite his strong stance, was to discover that he could not ignore the United States and the growing opposition to South African policies which developed in 1985. In 1984, the Reagan Administration's Assistant Secretary of State for Africa talked about 'constructive engagement' with the Republic, i.e. closer links with Pretoria. He believed that they were engaged in a policy of reform which was endorsed by a two to one white majority, but such reform would necessarily move slowly. Certain illusions, he felt, needed to be dispelled. First, that armed struggle would solve the problem; second, that South Africa faces a total onslaught from its neighbours; third, that South Africa will accept the UN resolution 435 on Namibia without a Cuban withdrawal from Angola and, finally, that South Africa will accept anything without getting something in return. The latter point is confirmed by the Nkomati accord which we have discussed above. But black voting power at the ballot box in America meant that the US administration had to think seriously about sanctions against the Republic in 1985. Restrictions were placed by Congress on future dealing between the International Monetary Fund and South Africa and there was pressure on local authorities to withdraw their pension funds from companies with investments in the Republic. The Democrats controlled the House of Representatives and members like Walter Mondale, Gary Hart and Jesse Jackson contended for economic, trading, security, and financial controls on Pretoria.

In this connection, the Secretary of State, Mr George Schultz, became a worried man, for the policy of 'constructive engagement' of 1984 seemed to be about to come apart. States such as

Nebraska, Columbia, Massachusetts, New York, California, were already considering or had already passed laws restricting public pension funds being invested in companies with interests in South Africa.

The Free South Africa Movement initiated demonstrations, anti-apartheid campaigns and demands that the so-called Sullivan principle, which pledges American firms in the Republic to work for equal pay and better conditions for their black South African employees, be tightened to commit them to lobby directly against apartheid. Despite arrests and threats, the movement continued its pressure on the Administration to apply sanctions against Pretoria. It was no surprise then that in 1985 it was decided that sanctions would be applied to the Republic to the extent that there would be a ban on the export or servicing of computers by US companies and the sale of gold Krugerrand coins in the US. US bank loans would be prohibited to the Republic and a bar erected on US private investment in the Republic or Namibia. But more was to follow in 1986.

The Eminent Persons Group was in the country in search of solutions to the South African problems when suddenly the South African Defence Force carried through strikes at ANC targets in Botswana, Zimbabwe and Zambia. Against a background of international anger towards the Republic, the US Congress overrode President Reagan's veto on further sanctions and imposed the most drastic penalties on the Republic ever adopted by an industrial nation to the extent that even South African Airways was denied the right to land in the country.

American policy towards South Africa in the eighties has moved from constructive engagement with Pretoria to drastic sanctions yet it had the continued worry about Cuban troops in Angola and the alleged communism of the ANC. However, in recent times there have been talks with the ANC, though nothing appears to have emerged from them, and there are moves to pump aid into the Front Line States to help alter their economic dependence on South Africa.

The relation with the US is very important for South Africa and I personally witnessed the gloom in the country when the strict sanctions were imposed, but there is also the desire to maintain good relations with Britain. A large proportion of the white population is English speaking and of British origin, and the interest in British affairs both by them and the Afrikaner continues to be prominent.

South Africa is bound to Britain by ties of history and blood and the economic link is a very strong one. The Republic is Britain's largest export market outside Europe and North America while Britain is South Africa's third largest overall export market. Britain is South Africa's largest investment partner with investments in the country of billions of rand.

When Mrs Thatcher came to power in 1979 she lifted the unofficial ban on the indirect sale of North Sea oil to the Republic but since then the relations have not been so cordial. Instances of strained relationships include: the suspicion that the Republic might be supplying arms to Argentina during the Falklands war, the expulsion of South African diplomats from Britain on the grounds of engaging in activities incompatible with their official status, the expulsion of Mr Joseph Klue of the military section of South African House for alleged spying and breaking into the London headquarters of SWAPO, and the war of words between Mr Botha and Mrs Thatcher which ended in the latter being told not to meddle in another country's affairs. Still, Mr Botha, despite protests by community councils and ethnic minority organizations did visit Britain in 1984, and met with Mrs Thatcher. Both in the press and interviews, he made certain that people here understood his point of view.

Fresh from the Nkomati agreement with Mozambique and unaware of how shaky its foundation was going to prove, he emphasized that such agreements showed the disenchantment of African states with the promises of the West. South Africa, he said, was not a threat to what we call the Front Line States and he earnestly desired to live in peace with them. However that may be, he then went on to try and demonstrate that the world was illogical in the way it regarded 'the homelands' of Transkei, Venda, Ciskei and Bophuthatswana, compared with Boswana, Lesotho and Swaziland. Why should recognition be given to the latter and not the former? Botswana, Lesotho and Swaziland had gained their emancipation from Britain in the post-colonial era, but they are now just as dependent on the Republic as the 'homelands' which South Africa emancipated. Moreover, his country is the largest supplier of aid in the African continent and has spent much money in Namibia and other African countries to relieve their poverty. He then went on to denounce the ANC which it was necessary to combat since it was communistic and the West must realize the threat to their interests posed by this organization which was backed by Russia. His government had initiated the new constitution for whites, coloured and Indians and this was a step on the road to power sharing for all races in the country.

He pleaded with Britain not to impose sanctions since this would damage trade between the two countries and if the raw materials from his country were stopped, thousands of jobs in British industry would be endangered. Throughout the speech, Botha emphasized that he wanted friendship with Britain and needed its help and support.

Reaction to this position taken up by the South African leader and government was mixed in 1985. Thus it was reported that the Foreign Office had confirmed that Britain bought a consignment of uranium from the Republic, reversing a ten-year official policy which ended contracts for South African uranium oxide. But, on the other hand, the TUC threatened to organize a pension fund boycott of ten British firms which failed to file reports under the EEC code of conduct on their South African subsidiaries' treatment of black workers. The International Confederation of Free Trade Unions which included the British TUC demanded that all new foreign investment in South Africa should stop and disinvestment be actively pursued.

There were difficulties here. British investments amounted to

£6 billion share portfolios and £5 billion in terms of money; British banks controlled 50% of the banking sector and many well-known British firms are investors and suppliers of practically everything from generators and electronics to computers. But mounting pressure against Pretoria has meant that a steady stream of foreign firms have withdrawn from the country during 1986 and 1987. On the 23 November 1986 Barclays Bank announced the sale of its interests in Barclays National Bank of South Africa to the Anglo American Corporation and associated companies; Allied Colloids, the R950 million British based industrial chemicals group, reported that they were selling their South African subsidiary to a local company; and on the 7 August 1987, Standard Chartered (UK) announced the sale of its 39% stake in its South African subsidiary Standard Bank Investment Corporation. But it has been the withdrawals of so many United States Corporations from the country that will hit the economy of the Republic the hardest blow.

The whole question of sanctions of course is a debatable issue and one that we cannot enter into here. Some firms believe that it is best to remain and try to better the lot of their black workers and bring pressure on the government to dismantle the apartheid system. BP Southern Africa, for example, the largest single British investor in South Africa, called for the abolition of apartheid in November, 1987, and provided R100 million to accelerate the process; and the previous month, Anglo-American reported its plan to build 24,000 low cost homes for black employees and their families and other industrialists said that they would be doing the same.

What can be said about sanctions is that they do damage the economy but it is doubtful whether they are effective as an overall strategy. Evidence can be produced to show that they are already damaging South African imports and exports and leading to unemployment in the country. Yet when internal surveys are taken regarding the opinions of the ordinary worker it is shown that some groups are for them and others against.

Since the US has imposed the most drastic sanctions we might mention that opinion there is still divided and that at the highest level. The report of the President in November 1987 admitted both the failure of constructive engagement and of sanctions to alter the thinking of Pretoria. Indeed, it went on to cast doubt on the external world's ability, short of armed invasion, to bring about a change to majority rule in South Africa. Senator Kennedy, on the other hand, criticized the report and argued that sanctions were working at least in the ferment which was being caused both in Afrikaner academic circles and the church. Thus the debate continues but, it should be noted, that Pretoria has been able to find loopholes even in US sanctions and has Japan now as its main trading partner.

Britain decided to oppose sanctions and for that reason has been isolated at recent Commonwealth conferences. Things would be different, of course, if the Labour Party was in power, for its dedication to the ANC cause is well known. Hence when Mr Oliver Tambo arrived in Britain he was warmly received by Mr Kinnock who embraced him on the Labour conference platform before a rapturous crowd. Mr Tambo said in his speech that sanctions were necessary, declared that Mrs Thatcher was out of touch with what was happening in his country, called for a one-man-one-vote in the Republic, said that whites would have nothing to fear under a black majority government, reminded the conference that Afrikaner unity was a thing of the past, stated that his liberation fighters did not want to inherit a land laid waste by war, and finished by seeking to demolish the argument that blacks would suffer through sanctions: 'We plead with you that you do not worry that we will, as a result, have to do without an evening meal. The stomachs of those who are shot down are empty already.' He called for the British people to impose sanctions themselves. At the debate however which took place on this issue division began to merge. One delegate argued that a composite resolution calling for the building of international links with South African workers to abolish capitalism and establish socialism was the product of the militant left wing of the Labour Party. Hence it was thought better to remit the resolution on this point for further consideration while they pushed ahead for a comprehensive strategy for sanctions and disinvestment. It is also worth noting that all the major churches in Britain have declared their support for sanctions.

Sanctions or not, South Africa's economic performance during the 1980s has been disappointing. Inflation averaged 14.6%, public sector expenditure rose from 19.5% in 1980 to 25.7% in 1986, the external value of the rand reached an all time low, interest rates increased, and unemployment began to rise. Gold, the heart of the Republic's economy, rose in price in 1982 but fell again during 1983 and 1984, the recession began to bite, and above all the socio-political environment had a detrimental effect on the economy.

In 1985, under the pressure of external sanctions, unrest, strikes in the gold mines, and the disappointing result of Botha's reform measures, the rand reached a value of 34.8 US cents. The stock exchange closed in August and did not reopen until the South African Reserve bank intervened in support of the currency. In September it was reported that the rand had gained about ten cents and that a financial rand had been introduced to prevent foreign investors from withdrawing their capital. This financial rand traded at a low dollar price and meant losses for those wishing to transfer their money overseas.

The Republic suspended repayment of its foreign debts until the end of 1985 when it was estimated that it had seventeen billion dollars of overseas debt. The moratorium did not affect interest payments for current imports and overseas bankers were confident that the country could repay its debt in due course. In April 1986 following an agreement between South Africa and its major creditor banks, a phase of partial repayment of foreign obligations began. A year later a new debt repayment schedule was agreed which extends until mid-1990.

The business section in the country startled by this debt and by the fact that Mr Gerhardus de Kock had been forced to use gold reserves as collateral to obtain international credit because some Western bankers had refused to renew loans, took the initiative to try and unlock the deadlock between Pretoria and the ANC. In due course they arranged a meeting with the ANC and put forward a proposal for a federal structure for the country which would be part of a new constitution but while they were received amicably by the organization it was apparent that the ANC thought Pretoria would eventually agree to majority rule. This belief has not been fulfilled for the state has by repressive measures under a state of emergency been able to contain the internal unrest and deal with its opponents abroad. It is still confident in 1989 that it can defeat the ANC.

In the next chapter we continue our personal experience of the country and try to understand what it is like to live in South Africa under such a state of emergency.

Chapter Five

A Divided Country

I arrived in Johannesburg in 1986 with a feeling of excitement mixed with fear. During the previous two years, the television in Europe and America had given viewers a nightly diet of bombings, shootings, riots and looting. Even in that most liberal city, Cape Town, whip-carrying policemen had been portrayed breaking up demonstrations; and in Durban blacks had engaged in ferocious tribal fighting. A state of emergency reigned in this beautiful sun-lit country.

But to my surprise, no troops were deployed around the airport which was filled with tourists and people visiting relatives. Business was being pursued as normal and, apart from an occasional bomb in a supermarket or night club in one of the bigger cities and the bad news about South Africa from abroad, one might have wondered what all the furore was about. This is one of the deceptive features of life in the Republic. As long as you stay in the white areas, which means the main centre of towns and cities, and don't stray into the black townships, you could be deceived into thinking that all was well.

I was determined, however, to discover how the ordinary person had experienced these years of violence and what he thought of how the media had reported it. This, at least, would make a change from the interviewing of leading black politicians and clergymen by their counterparts in Britain and America who arrived on 'lightning' tours of the country. Such visits reminded me of the American who visited Ulster for a couple of days and arrived back home with the right answers to all the problems of that conflict!

I took the train from Johannesburg to Pretoria and started to talk to as many people as would talk to me! A young white who was working in a supermarket called 'Checkers' complained that his parents in Zimbabwe couldn't get their money out of the country. He alleged that discrimination against whites in that country was worse than white against black in the Republic. He wanted to stay in South Africa, but was having difficulty in getting a resident permit. I expressed surprise for I had thought that the country would have wanted to increase its white population since it had about 20 million blacks. But he explained that jobs for the unskilled were hard to get.

The blacks were segregated into another part of the train but, though it was against the rules, I ventured into their area. Since the media had given me the impression that there was unbelievable tension between black and white, I had expected scowls, but was greeted with welcoming smiles. If these people were revolutionaries, they certainly had the ability to disguise the fact! Actually during this year in South Africa, I found the Africans to be very helpful, even to the extent of pushing my car when it broke down a number of times in the course of my journeys. I engaged a well-dressed middle-class black in conversation. His complaint was that he had to travel in these overcrowded compartments when he had the money to pay the first class fare for a seat in the white section. The same applied to housing. Why should he have to live in the black township of Soweto and be excluded from buying a house in the white suburbs of Johannesburg? If the Prime Minister believed that apartheid was outdated, then he ought to remove the Group Areas Act which separated the races into different residential areas.

By this time, the guard was indicating to me that I was travelling in the wrong part of the train and had better move to my own place. But, as I left, I could not help observing that the majority of the blacks were better dressed and looked healthier than the blacks that I had seen in the cities of Nigeria.

A Portuguese taxi driver drove me to the South African Broadcasting House, where I was scheduled to give an interview. He had lived for thirty years in Johannesburg and was convinced that the overseas media had been biased in its reportage, focussing on sensational incidents and not reporting the normality of the country in general. Further, he alleged that some people had been bribed to create sensational news cover. I reminded him that newspapers and television had demanded evidence for this, but none had been forthcoming. 'How can they get evidence,' he protested, 'as soon as the police or army arrives, those who had initially caused the trouble, have disappeared.' I was sceptical about all of this, but later the Principal of a College confirmed it by pointing out that children had been televised outside a school to give the impression that they had been locked out by the apartheid laws. Like most schools, it had to be locked at certain times in the day for security reasons, but children had been bribed to congregate at those times.

I lunched in a city restaurant and asked the proprietor about his customers. He said that there was now a much greater relaxation of apartheid laws, and that hotels and restaurants were now admitting all races. He had always done this and had never had any trouble. He, too, thought the press reports about the troubles had been exaggerated, but admitted tension between the army and riot police in dealing with them. The latter were often brutal in their methods of arrest and interrogation whereas the army in the townships was largely composed of young lads doing their national service. Since they had generally a good relation with the blacks on their farms and in their towns, they were surprised and appalled by some of the scenes that they had witnessed.

In the afternoon, I had a long discussion with a leading churchman, who complained about Botha's refusal to talk with the African National Congress. He had written a letter to Botha and had received the reply that his government, a Christian government, did not negotiate with terrorists. I asked: 'Why does the ANC not renounce violence, at least for a period of time, and talk with Botha? If they did, and Botha still refused to negotiate, he would be condemned by world opinion and moderate whites in the country.' I added that perhaps he might write a letter to the ANC suggesting this! Of course the ANC would say that it does not unilaterally renounce violence because the state refuses to renounce violence which created the situation of injustice in the first place.

I made my way back to the railway station in pouring rain (the brochures do not mention this) and was confronted by 'petty apartheid' in the form of separate toilets and telephone booths. But the law was being observed, 'in the breach rather than in the observance', for the whites, having more money and needing to make more telephone calls, had invaded the black booths.

As I approached the toilets, I noticed one labelled blanks which I mistook for blacks, but then realized as whites came out, that blanks was Afrikaans for white. Being more sure of my ground, I ventured in but was puzzled by a black man preceding me. Suddenly, realizing his mistake, he laughingly turned round and went towards the black one. I think this humour of the blacks may yet prove a saving grace in South Africa. It reminded me of what I had seen on television the previous evening. At a meeting in celebration of South African sport, where much was made of the races playing together, an eminent black speaker was introduced. He told the story of the bishop who was asking God when an Indian would be Prime Minister of the country. God replied: 'Not in your lifetime.' He repeated the question about a coloured man (mixed race) and got the same answer. Then came the important question: 'When will a black man be Prime Minister?' God replied: 'Not in *my* life time'!

I alighted from the train at a station on the outskirts of Pretoria called 'Verwoerdburg' (after Dr Verwoerd, who instituted apartheid in 1948) and discovered two hard-line Afrikaners sitting on a seat under the sign! They did not 'mince their words': 'These bloody blacks, they want to rule the world. If General Smuts were here now, he would soon have put a stop to their nonsense. It is Botha's fault with his reforms, if only he had left things alone.' The reference was to the tri-racial Parliament, which Botha had instituted consisting of Indians, coloured and whites, but leaving out the blacks. This had fuelled the unrest in 1984 and 1985.

Later, I spoke to a black clergyman who had ministered in the townships in Pretoria. 'Blacks want liberation,' he said, 'but often show that they are not ready for it.' He feared that majority rule would cause many whites to leave the country, and the place could deteriorate into a third world country. He smiled: 'Your British taxpayers would not want that.' Things were bad in the townships, he said, because the people would not accept the local councils approved by the state; and there was much intimidation by the ANC, which forced them to boycott white shops. 'Yet, the comrades, as they call themselves, do nothing about the traders in the townships who exploit the people with their high prices.' We were chatting in the main street, when two prosperous blacks emerged from a white shop and hurried to their Mercedes. 'You see,' he remarked, 'they have to hurry, for if the comrades got them, they would burn their car and perhaps them as well!'

What strikes the visitors forcibly is the mass of blacks crowding the streets of the towns and cities. Since many are unemployed, the crime rate is high. This breeds a feeling of insecurity among the whites, and many protect their homes with savage dogs and the latest burglar-proofing. One evening, I was dining at a restaurant with a friend when there was the noise of conflict in the kitchen. One of the black cooks staggered out with blood streaming down her face. She had been attacked by another black worker. Panic quickly showed itself among the whites, although the black security forces were at hand. Some hurried from the place, leaving their meal untouched while others stood nervously around, not knowing what to do.

But the black servants in the hotel where I stayed were friendly and more polite than I have experienced in Britain. They were anxious to please and grateful for any gratuity. There was no segregation of black and white residents.

I taught in the university whites from all over the country and Africans, mainly Zulus and Xhosa. The Zulus were very lively and encouraged me to visit their own university which was in Zululand. The Xhosa spoke quite openly about the trouble in their townships and the fears and hopes of their people. Most trouble seems to start with arrests by the police and the brutality of the riot squads. Often a funeral fuelled the unrest. This was as much a political gathering as a religious service, and speakers from the ANC were often prominent. 'You must understand,' the Xhosas said, 'that religion and politics are so intertwined, that it is impossible to separate them. Both speak for the liberation of the people.'

An example of trouble at a funeral occurred at Joza, near Grahamstown. It was for a high school pupil who had been shot by police at a funeral two weeks previously. A crowd gathered at 10 am in a stadium and were addressed by a stream of speakers, which included a prominent member of the United Democratic Front. There were about 4,000 people present, with many more prevented from attending by the local magistrate, who had issued orders that only relatives and friends should be allowed to come. The MP for the district of Albany and the black and white Ministers' Fraternal attended. This was fortunate, for once the rioting started, they were able to act as mediators between the police and the blacks. I talked with one of the black workers, who arrived the following day at the university, covered with bruises.

She was usually happy and polite, but on that day, she was really annoyed and showed bitter resentment against the riot police. 'They couldn't wait for even a few minutes when the crowd had not dispersed at the agreed time of 2 pm, but immediately lobbed teargas into the procession, causing panic and confusion.' She, with many others, had been knocked to the ground and trampled underfoot. A Methodist minister who had been present told me that when he and his colleagues from the Ministers' Fraternal had sought to intercede, they had been jeered at by the police, and had teargas thrown at them. One minister had collapsed, and another saw a young woman being struck with a rifle. A boy of about six months suffocated from the gas, and five other people had been injured. The MP said that he would present a full report of the funeral to the minister of Law and Order, Mr Louis le Grange, and confirmed that all had been peaceful until the police intervened.

This provocative attitude of the police contrasts sharply with what was happening in governmental circles at this time. The state of emergency had been lifted and in April, President P. W. Botha issued his programme of reforms. In the newspapers the following statement appeared:

INFLUX CONTROL HAS BEEN ABOLISHED

THE PASS LAWS HAVE GONE

THE PRISONS ARE EMPTIED OF THE VICTIMS OF THIS UNHAPPY SYSTEM

NO SOUTH AFRICAN WILL EVER SUFFER THE INDIGNITY OF ARREST FOR A PASS OFFENCE AGAIN

A NEW ERA OF FREEDOM HAS BEGUN

These basically meant that Africans would no longer be restricted in their movements, and would be able to go anywhere to find work. Under the pass laws, the blacks had to have passes in order to prove that they were entitled to be in a particular area. Later, Botha announced the introduction of uniform identity documents for all South Africans instead of the passes which only blacks had to carry in the past. In July, the four whites-only provincial councils were replaced by multi-racial regional councils and provincial executive councils. These would be the second tier of government, and were intended to act as a example of what could happen at the first-tier. The blacks had representation on the provincial executive committees for the first time in the history of South Africa.

In the April notice, Botha continued: 'When I made the promise to scrap the pass laws by July 1, a new spirit of optimism was felt throughout the land. Now that promise has been fulfilled, and the lies and accusations of those who said it would never happen have been proved as empty as the cruel and selfish ideologies they would force upon an unwilling nation. We are a land of many groups, each with a right to protection, each with a right to share in the prosperity of the greatest nation in Africa. To those skulking criminals who sneak around at night, killing and maiming innocent people in the most cowardly way, I say beware. The new South Africa will be a land where all decent people can sleep with their doors open. A land where we can look each other in the eye, without fear or hatred. And it will come about. Not because I say so, but because my government and I have the power to make it happen. That is the reality. The time for retribution is over. Yes, it is the time for all South Africans to act like men. Not lie snivelling with their heads under their pillows. It is time to stretch out our hand and look each other squarely in the eyes, around the negotiating table . . . You have seen that in my hands, negotiation is the most powerful weapon of all. But I will not suffer the slaughter of innocents. I will not contemplate any path towards change other than change through peaceful evolution. This, I can promise you: when the history of the new South Africa is written, it will not be in blood. It will be written in the one thing our enemies fear the most – peace and goodwill.'

Anti-apartheid leaders recognized that the repeal of the pass laws was a substantial change, but the blacks appointed to the provincial committees were government nominees and not elected, and this was not acceptable. These reforms were followed by the repeal of the Mixed Marriages and Immorality Acts which prevented people of different races marrying; freehold land tenure (land could be acquired by urban blacks); and access by black businessmen to central districts.

I asked the black students why the unrest continued in the light of these reforms. They said that many legitimate black leaders who should be involved in negotiations with government were not available for participation, e.g. Nelson Mandela. Separate education is still there, though at university level many white universities have admitted black students. Multi-racial schools, too, are to be envisaged. The big demand, however, is for universal sufferage, which a state struggling towards possible power-sharing will not even consider.

As the anniversary of Soweto approached in June, rumours of a national rising caused the re-imposition of the state of emergency. One of my friends refused to meet me at the Johannesburg airport as he was convinced that 20,000 blacks were going to march on Pretoria, but when I travelled there on the 16, I hardly saw a black person, and it was business as usual in the city.

As the year proceeded, however, the big news was sanctions. The *Today* programme on SABC discussed and speculated on the debate in America, Britain and Europe. Eventually, Reagan was over-ruled by the Senate, and South Africa heard the worst. Britain tried harder with the visit of Sir Geoffrey Howe, but the South African government refused to release Nelson Mandela and talk with the ANC until violence was renounced.

Many blacks argued that they were willing to suffer sanctions with the consequences of higher unemployment and poverty, but others like Chief Buthelezi of the Zulus thought that they would not have the desired effect. It is argued that sanctions will make the Afrikaner harder and more repressive, for restraint apart from any internal moral consideration will have been removed. The Afrikaner says that all the new reforms which Botha has instituted have only led to greater demands. In the short term he can survive, even create greater employment with the cuts in imports, but in the long term, with the country incapable of further economic growth, the outlook is bleak. Certainly, the West needs to think hard about the long-term consequences of such sanctions. It cannot want, after relieving famine in sub-Saharan Africa, to bring about another Ethiopia in the South, for it is not only the Republic that will be affected, but all the neighbouring states who are now dependent upon the South African economy.

A DIVIDED COUNTRY

What kind of South Africa would the majority eventually inherit?

The right-wing Afrikaner tells the more moderate that he has always argued that concessions to the morality of the West will bring disaster. This is not his way. I attended a local meeting of the Conservative Party, and heard the message of strong resistance against any multi-racial society. The solution, the speaker said, was on the basis of a partition of the country into different ethnic groupings. If their party came to power, new homelands would be created for the coloured and Indians and the whites, and they would have their rights there. This attitude stemmed from a traditional argument for racial purity and a seige mentality reinforced by sanctions.

One of the fascinating things in the country which often goes unnoticed by the media is the relationship between the domestic servants and their employers. What they receive from their mistresses cannot be measured by their basic wages. One woman said to me about her black maid: 'I have seen her through widowhood, an illegitimate child, an illegitimate grandchild, schoolbooks and fees, funerals and illness.' This was not exaggerated or related simply to one case. I heard of many acts of paternalism and observed the tremendous generosity of a friend's wife. She ordered meat for the maid and gardener every day, paid bus fares, supplied them with bread, milk and vegetables, and was always ready with cash for emergencies. Two of the maid's sons and one daughter had had their education paid for them and one of the sons, having done well, was sent by them to America for further education. She never referred to the Africans as servants, but spoke of the needs of the family.

In the black townships, social unrest and unemployment were having their effect on family life. Social workers reported heavy drinking on the part of unemployed men and wives were overburdened with work and responsibility. Parents were losing interest in their children, not only because of their own worries, but through failure to control them. The old tradition of respect for elders seemed to be breaking down, with youths roaming the townships in revolt against all authority. Schools were closed because of boycotts and children did not know what to do with their time. Some children that I knew personally told me that when they attempted to go to school, they were chased away by the comrades. Attacks continued on local black councillors and their families. There were reports of stabbings and killings and the burning of homes. One of the most extreme acts of violence was the killing of the twelve-year-old son of a councillor, who was hacked to death by five men.

Students at the universities of Cape Town, Witwatersrand, Natal and Rhodes, spearheaded initiatives by the National Union of Students to have talks with the ANC. The main argument for such a move was that discussions with this banned organization on the part of the Progressive Federal Party, the English business section, and the Church of the Province of South Africa, had been profitable. The students argued that the Nationalist's refusal to talk to the ANC because of their violence was invalid, for the ANC had been driven to that strategy. It was essential to talk to the ANC because of its support both at home and abroad.

These are English-speaking universities, however, and do not represent the Afrikaner's institutions. During my last two periods in the country I had spoken at Stellenbosch and Pretoria and quickly realized that here there was a dedication to and commitment to past history which had formed current beliefs and values. Determined to find out more about these values, I travelled by car to one of the strongholds of Afrikanerdom: Bloemfontein in the Orange Free State. Fleeing in 1806 from an alien administration at the Cape, the Afrikaners settled in Natal, the Orange Free State and the Transvaal. Even there, they were not safe for the British followed and conquered them: Natal (1842), Transvaal (1877), and the Orange Free State (during the Boer War of 1899–1902). At the University of Bloemfontein there is a great stress on history, with a complete section dedicated to the memory of Dr Verwoerd who instituted apartheid in 1948. But in the nineteenth century the Boer became a guerrilla fighter after he had been defeated in open conflict with the British. A black of today would heartily agree with the Boer's sentiments: 'Too noble is the blood, too free, to lie in the bonds of slavery . . .' The Afrikaner knows too well the blacks' aspirations, for he was a freedom fighter against the British and the Women's Memorial and the War Museum of the Boer Republic testify to this fact. It was only the appalling conditions of the concentration camps where the mothers and children were interned by the British that brought the guerrilla fighters to the negotiating table, and the Peace of Vereeniging was signed on 31 May 1902.

The guerrillas feared that their nation would die out if the high death rate in the camps was not brought to an end. And, with the scorched earth policy of the British, they were on the verge of starvation. Accommodation at the camps was very uncomfortable, sanitation was inadequate, and measles and whooping cough reached epidemic proportions. In the Bloemfontein camp, more than half the inhabitants had to sleep on the ground without blankets. They were exposed to cold and rain, poor clothing, inadequate food and bad medical services, so that a large percentage died. The total figure in these camps that died is estimated at 27,927, of whom 22,074 were children below the age of sixteen.

It is an episode which has dishonoured the name of Britain and made the Afrikaner suspicious of the English. But the history drives home the point that it is not the first time that he has had his back against the wall and yet has survived to build the best nation economically on the African continent. This gives him a faith, not only in his people, but in God. As the Revd J. D. Kestell wrote: 'God moulded the Afrikaner nation in this great struggle. It was not vanquished. Its language was not destroyed; no sword can suppress its spirit. The Afrikaner nation remains an unconquerable element . . .'

It is this past which makes the modern Afrikaner, especially the right-winger, believe that he can still survive even if he is threatened and isolated by the rest of the world. Indeed, external pressure could drive him more and more into his laager. At times he even doubts that the West will listen to his defence and what he is trying to do for the blacks. Crossroads, the squatter camp, is an example of this. I visited it myself in 1981, and saw the appalling conditions, but in 1986 fighting broke out between the comrades and other blacks there. Many were injured and killed and this included reporters from the overseas media. On seeing the poverty and squalor, Mrs Coretta King, widow of the Civil Rights leader Dr Martin Luther King exclaimed: 'Even knowing slum conditions in my own country, this defies the imagination . . .' 'It's tragic . . .' commented Archbishop Edmund Browning, Bishop of the American Church. 'I pray to God that these people will soon be moved to decent housing . . .' said Dr Robert Runcie, Archbishop of Canterbury. But, says the Afrikaner, these visitors on their 'lightning tour' neglected to travel eight kilometres further south to see the new town of Khayelitsha which is being built for 250,000 people. Here is a modern lay-out consisting of clinics, schools, community centres and shopping complexes. In July 1986, at the time of their visit, about 35,000 people were living in 5,000 houses and around 120,000 had settled on the site-and-service plots adjacent to Khayelitsha. These plots are free, while the houses can be bought for R.8,000 or rented for R.20 per month. There are play parks, sports fields, green open spaces, tree-lined streets, and a giant swimming pool. It is hard to understand why some 'human rights' campaigners try to discourage the people from moving here, and it is even more difficult to understand why this group of visitors did not find time to visit it.

The Afrikaner is right when he says that there are always two sides to every argument, and at times the world refuses to listen to their side of the case. Thus Mrs King listened to Dr Allan Boesak, Archbishop Desmond Tutu, and Mrs Winnie Mandela, but did not keep her appointment with the State President.

On the other hand, the Afrikaner has lost a lot of world sympathy by his clamping down on free speech and detaining leaders of the people who oppose his administration. Information about detainees is becoming increasingly difficult to obtain and their numbers rose to over 8,000 in 1986. Court case rulings indicate that many had been detained without sufficient evidence and that conditions in prison were bad with as many as six in a cell. Long interrogation, isolation from family and friends, and being held for days without access to reasonable ablution facilities or change of clothes or proper medication . . . all pointed to the Afrikaner now doing things to others what had been done to him in years past.

On the home front, the Afrikaner is having difficulty in convincing the young whites that they should, under the present circumstances, fight for their country and that conscription is the best way of doing it. An End Conscription Campaign has been under way for a number of years, with centres all over the country. It has the backing of a number of academics, politicians and clergy, and argues that individuals should be free to choose whether or not to serve in the South African Defence Force. Under the emergency regulations, however, the state has introduced a ban on anyone opposing compulsory military service with the penalty for contravening the regulations of a possible ten years in prison or a fine of R.20,000. Consequently, at least fifty ECC members have been detained and their homes raided for literature. The conscripts disliked in particular their work in the townships, but were compelled to do it. In 1985 there were about 35,000 SADF troops deployed in ninety-three townships. The organization believes that such a presence only exacerbates conflict, whereas community projects undertaken by the ECC such as first-aid classes, planting of trees and crops, holiday programmes, planting of parks and painting of hospital wards, contributed to peace and reconciliation. It is this kind of service instead of military that should be considered by the state. Figures released in Parliament showed that in 1984-5 7,589 people failed to report for national service.

It is impossible, however, to understand the actions of the Afrikaner and his imposition of states of emergency etc. without a realization of the goals and objectives of the force that he is fighting: the ANC. This organization started on peaceful lines, but then moved to violence. Its military wing came into existence on 16 December 1961 and is called Umkhonto we Sizwo. Its manifesto states that they were forced into violence because non-violence was interpreted by the state as a sign of weakness. Its goal, which is intended to bring happiness to all people in the country, black, brown and white, is the overthrow of the state, the abolition of white supremacy, and the winning of liberty, democracy, and full national rights and equality for all.

The ANC has a freedom Charter which stresses:

The people shall govern
All national groups shall have equal rights
The people shall share in the country's wealth
The land shall be shared among those who work it
All shall be equal before the law
All shall enjoy equal human rights
There shall be work and security
The doors of learning and of culture shall be opened
There shall be houses, security and comfort
There shall be peace and friendship

The implications of these are: majority rule, all apartheid laws set aside, all banks and industry shall be transferred to the people, the land redivided among the workers, the state will supply the equipment to work the land, freedom of movement will be guaranteed, the police force and army will be open to all, free trade unions will be formed, there shall be equal pay for equal work, education will be free, compulsory, universal and equal for all children, higher education will be open to all on the basis of merit, rent and prices for housing and goods shall be lowered, there will be free medical care, slums will be demolished, and South Africa will be a fully independent state dedicated to maintaining world peace by negotiation, not war.

A DIVIDED COUNTRY

It is a devastating social programme which ought to make the capitalist, not only in South Africa, but in the West, sit up and take notice! In his message to the National Executive Committee of the ANC on 8 January 1986, Comrade President Oliver Tambo outlined the strategy for 1986. A crucial day in 1986, he said, would be the tenth anniversary of the Soweto Uprising and, therefore, 16 June would be recognized as South African Youth Day. Such a forecast of trouble was treated so seriously by the authorities, that they responded by re-introducing the state of emergency just before 16 June. Thus, the day passed with little incident.

Tambo went on in his speech to welcome the formation of the Congress of South African Trade Unions and appealed to all unions to join it, for it represented the solidarity of the working class. He said that May Day, international workers' solidarity day, must be celebrated in the country as a holiday, and in the event thousands, despite the protests of their employers, stayed away from work.

He recognized with pride that revolutionary young people had emerged from the masses and that the struggle was now a people's war. He called on white compatriots to break ranks with the system and to refuse service in the armed forces. Black and white, as equals, could build a new state. He discounted rumours of secret talks with the Botha regime but said that discussions would continue with the business sector and all sections of industry. He called for an end to the pass laws, and this, we have noted, did happen during the year; but his call to release all political prisoners and detainees unconditionally went undeeded.

Tambo envisaged the destruction of the puppet local councils set up by the state, and the arousing of world opinion regarding the struggle in South Africa and the introduction of sanctions. It is a measure of the strength of his organization that this was brought about and confirmed his claim that the ANC is stronger than ever before.

He said that 1986 would be the year of the People's Army and would celebrate the 25th anniversary of the formation of their military wing: Umkhonto we Sizwe. Again, what he intended on 16 December, as on 16 June, did not take place, for further draconian measures against the ANC supporters and the press were introduced by the state following Botha's speech to the nation on 12 December.

Important questions were put to Tambo at a press conference in Luska on 9 January 1986 which clarify the position of his organization; we mention some of them. An interesting one was how the ANC intended to make the country ungovernable. Tambo said that the first move was to destroy the local structure of the system on which it was intended to build a constitutional order to serve urban Africans. He might have had in mind here the idea of making Soweto into a black satellite city with its own administration and council control. Tambo opposed constitutional provisions for separate groups in the country which he sees as planning along the usual apartheid plan. Thus the people called upon the local councillors to resign, and when some of them did not, they were attacked. It is likely that this attack was mounted by what Tambo calls combat units (ANC members) who compelled the majority to do what they wanted. Questioned about the effect of this, that black would then be against black, he said that this had not been their intention and that it was incidental. But in the eyes of the world, such 'necklacing' (burning tyre round the neck of the victim) was not 'incidental'.

Questioned about the bomb at Amanzimtoti before Christmas 1985, Tambo was evasive, though the question came up a number of times. He said that they did not know yet who was responsible, but whites (a number were killed and injured) could expect death in a war where civilians get caught in the cross-fire. In the light of the fact that so many blacks had been killed in the townships, the whites could expect to find the same thing happening in their areas. Pressed again, Tambo said: 'I cannot be answerable for every little thing that happens . . .' The reason for his embarrassment was that the ANC had said that they would not attack 'soft targets'; but it may also indicate a split in the organization as happened with the IRA in Ulster. Tambo, however, denied this.

Another important question was whether or not the ANC would be willing to put a moratorium on violence in order to negotiate with the state. Tambo said the first step would be the release of Nelson Mandela but it was really not necessary for a moratorium before serious talks began and it could come about at some stage in the talks. The ANC could stop its armed struggle but it is against the violence and injustice of apartheid ... 'Would the regime be able to stop the violence of the apartheid system? We don't see how they would do that. But theoretically, it can be done, because theoretically, the regime can take steps to put an end to the apartheid system ... They can take bold initiatives which would convince everybody that now we have reached the end of the apartheid system, and we need only now negotiate the mechanisms for the transfer of power.'

Tambo then makes no secret of the fact that the goal of the ANC is the attainment of power in the Republic, and at various other meetings and conferences in 1985 and 1986 he made this very clear. Those nations and countries which have supported the ANC in their struggle are praised and imperialistic countries, such as the United States of America, derided. He sees the USA as the leader of world imperialism and cites Vietnam and South America as examples of its strategy. The main aim of these conferences, however, was to try to resolve disunity which had crept into the ranks and to reconcile differences with other black organizations such as the Pan African Congress, the African Nationalists and the Black Consciousness movements. These were too racial and failed to understand that this was a class struggle as well as a racial one. Socialist countries are praised continually for the help which they have given over the years and their fight against United States' imperialism.

Further, in its desire for unity, the ANC is encouraged by the United Democratic Front organization which admits all races to its membership; and by the resistance offered to the apartheid regime by the coloureds. The reference is to the coloureds of the

Cape who rejected the triracial parliament and engaged in violent clashes with the police and the education authorities in 1985.

This brief survey of the ideas of the ANC shows that they are putting forward demands which given the implacability of the government cannot be realized without the most bloody civil war in the history of the African continent. But we have also noticed a certain willingness to negotiate, and the more radical demands may simply be a prelude to a compromise settlement which would involve some sort of power-sharing. Otherwise, the position is one of total confrontation since the Afrikaner is just as determined to hold on what he has got and fight to the end for it. The only hope of avoiding civil war is that moderates on both sides may be able to persuade the more radical and violent elements to compromise.

Tambo and his organization need to face the fact that the conflict is not only with the whites but that blacks in the country are divided. This became clear in the press conference when the question was put to him about the position of Chief Buthelezi, the Zulu leader. He was asked if the rift with Buthelezi could be mended: 'Well, of course, there is nothing at the moment to suggest that it can be or that it is going to be. Let me put it that way... It is Chief Buthelezi who is fighting his own battle against the ANC. But the ANC is too pre-occupied with the struggle to take much notice of what he is saying.'

Can Tambo 'write off' Buthelezi so easily? The Zulus have always been the most warlike of the tribes and, if the ANC dream of ending white rule was an accomplished fact, would the Zulus submit to ANC leadership? The thought of a civil war between the black groups cannot be set aside, and I would hesitate to think of this awful conflict since I was present in Nigeria during the time of the civil war between Yoruba and Ibo. The whole scenario raises the question of the use of violence and how a prosperous and peaceful country can emerge from such a conflict.

However that may be, I was determined to see what the Zulus were like on their 'home ground', and had the opportunity of visiting the University of Zululand later in the year. It has a rural setting about 350 kilometres south west of the very well-developed seaside resort of Richards Bay and 150 kilometres to the north of Durban. Initially, only Zulu and Swazi were admitted, but since 1985, the university has been open to all races. It has very impressive buildings, a lovely location, and an experienced and well-equipped staff. One of its goals is to act as an instrument of change and to be a catalyst in removing the imbalances that exist in South African society. I delivered lectures to the staff and students in a crowded auditorium, and was impressed by their attention and the questions that they asked afterwards. I think it is the vitality and enthusiasm of the Zulus that I like and their respect for traditions.

I remember in one of my classes at Rhodes University in Grahamstown, a Zulu appeared one day in a very expensive suit and when I asked him why he was so well attired, he said that it was his mother's birthday. I was puzzled since he was far from home and would be unable to attend the celebration. 'I know,' he said, 'but I will 'phone her and tell her that I am celebrating the occasion properly here!' I wondered what the Xhosas in the class thought of this since their elders were currently bemoaning the lack of respect in young people for their parents.

Chief Buthelezi is the Chancellor of the University and is greatly respected by the students and Zulu people in general. They are more than a quarter of the African population of the Republic, and live in a large part of the province of Natal which is called KwaZulu. Buthelezi condemns apartheid and has consistently refused to accept 'homeland' status for his area, but he is determined to work within the system in order to reform it.

In July 1986, he addressed a large rally in Soweto and announced that he was willing to accept a place on the government's National Council as a forum for negotiating a power-sharing scheme. His Zulu Inkatha movement is a rival to the ANC and, though in his speech he called for the release of Nelson Mandela, his refusal to use violence and his decision to work with the state in the process of reform has alienated him from them. He contends that sanctions will only bring more poverty and conflict to the country so he opposes them. On the positive side, he has been instrumental in the scheme for power-sharing between the Zulus, whites and Indians of Natal and sees it as a model for the rest of the country. Such a scheme would be opposed by the ANC, but currently it is the right-wing Afrikaner who opposes such multi-racial government for Natal because he fears it might lead to an alliance of the English-speaking whites and the others against himself.

After the visit to Zululand, I wanted to see Lesotho and have a quick look at Bophuthatswana. I left Grahamstown to drive via Port Beaufort and Jamestown. Outside Jamestown, I parked for lunch in one of those lovely lay-bys which abound on the South African roads but when I tried to start the car there were no signs of life. I was puzzled about this for I had bought a new battery on the way to Bloemfontein. Fortunately, it was parked on a slope and with the help of a passing motorist, I managed to reach a garage in Jamestown, but they could not fix it and I had to travel on to Aliwal North. Unfortunately, the car stopped at the lights in the middle of the town and I had to hop out and persuade the occupants of another car to give it a push. Four well-dressed blacks readily yielded to my persuasion and after a push it started again. I was very grateful to the blacks and this act showed me again how ready they were to help.

The next morning I drove for twenty kilometres over a road very much in need of repair, and then discovered that I had left my coat in the hotel. I could not think of returning over the bad road and decided that Lesotho University would have to put up with a pullover-clad lecturer. In the event, they were very informal and didn't even comment.

I wondered about so little repair work going on and thought it might be a sign that the economic depression was hitting the Republic. But I was to lose my dissatisfaction with these roads in South Africa when I compared them with the awful state of those in Lesotho. There the roads had huge potholes and I shuddered with fear that the car would collapse on the way to Roma where the university is situated. Broken-down vehicles of every description lay at the side of the road, with most of them having had their parts removed. The people of Maseru, the capital and only city of any size, reminded me of the Nigerians as they strolled across the road to the accompaniment of loud hooting or bartered by the roadside for all kinds of goods. There was much laughter, shouting and friendliness even though the rain was streaming down. A poor country but to all appearances, a happy one.

Lesotho is one of the three kingdoms of Africa (the others are Morocco and Swaziland) and was a British Protectorate from 1868 to 1966. It gained its independence on 4 October 1966, and from 1970–1986 was ruled in a dictatorial way by Leabua Jonathan. Since 20 January 1986, after the South African blockade, it has been under a military regime which is determined to co-operate with Pretoria. Such African dictatorships and military regimes do not apparently incur the same wrath as the apartheid system of South Africa, for every kind of external aid is extended to Lesotho from the United States Food agencies to the American peace corps. Mainly an agricultural land, it did experiment with a diamond mine, but this has now been closed down. There is little industry and tourism is experiencing great difficulties. Most things are imported from the Republic and 117,000 of the men have migrated to that country in order to work in the mines.

The Catholic church has an extensive mission throughout the country with four dioceses, three central missions and 419 outstations. It is heavily involved in education and in the hospital services. I stayed with the Catholic fathers at the university and admired their beautiful chapel which has a central place on the campus. There are excellent facilities for the students and the site at Roma is impressive, being surrounded by a barrier of rugged mountains which provide magnificent scenery. The students crowded the lecture rooms to hear what I had to say and were very quick to ask questions if they did not understand something.

It is this enthusiasm for learning which impresses me about the blacks and which I first noticed in Nigeria. Perhaps it is due to the struggle which they have to undergo in order to get to university that makes them so keen to take advantage of what it has to offer.

Bophuthatswana lies close to Lesotho and I decided to pay it a quick visit. Unlike Lesotho it is a South African homeland and does not enjoy the approval of the world or the aid that it can offer, but apartheid does not exist here and there is rapid economic growth. The capital Mmabatho and the new airport at Garona are impressive and busy; industry, tourism and mining are flourishing and everyone has the right to vote. Black government officials asserted that they accepted independence because it meant getting back the land which had belonged to their forefathers and the right to govern themselves. It was, they said, much better to seize the opportunity when it came than continue to live under apartheid. 'Sun city' (some puritans in South Africa call it 'sin city') is the entertainment capital of the land and attracts thousands of tourists. In early February 1988 there was a coup in the country but South Africa immediately intervened and had no difficulty in restoring President Lucas Mangope to power. Here, black and white mingle happily together and show, in this part of Southern Africa, that there is no need for the races to be divided. Bophuthatswana appears to be the most successful homeland that I have seen, and one wonders if they would not oppose the ANC view that such homelands must be dismantled when majority rule takes over in South Africa. It would seem that the Zulus may not be the only obstacle in such a plan.

Returning to South Africa with some difficulty as the border customs between Lesotho and the Republic are very stringent on the South African side, I found the vice-chancellors of the English-speaking universities calling for a lifting of the state of emergency. Their statement argued that universities cannot carry out their work properly because restricted access to information prevents investigation and research in many areas. The definition of prohibited 'subversive statements' is so broad that critical discussions and analysis is seriously curtailed. Further, provision for the searching of premises and for the seizure of materials and documents allows access without warrant to private papers and confidential records. Detention without charge or trial (it needs to be mentioned that a large number of university personnel have been detained) allows for the intimidation and arrest of staff and students for the opinions they form in the pursuit of their legitimate educational objectives. The statement then went on to make courageously points that must have been regarded by the state as subversive. 'We are deeply concerned that the principles of justice have been subverted in relation to the above matters and we are further concerned that what is happening in South Africa at the moment is reflecting not only on students but also on the careers of thousands of schoolchildren. Pupils have been detained in large numbers and regulations recently announced by the Department of Education and Training have had a profoundly negative effect on schools which feed our universities. The education of our prospective students has, thus, been placed in jeopardy ... It is our view that the current crisis is a product of delay in extending basic political and civil rights to the majority of the population and that in this situation, violence has escalated and black education has become a focus, a symbol and a cause for the most serious social unrest ... We call upon all to desist from violence and upon the government to lift the state of emergency, and to release all detainees or charge them in a court of law ... and to address the problems in black education immediately and imaginatively without measures as drastic as those currently in force, but through negotiation and with a receptive spirit.'

This courageous statement was a strong message, not only for the state in South Africa, but for the external universities and unions overseas who have insisted on a boycott of academics from South Africa. It is difficult to understand how those people living so far away from these problems can seek to isolate academics and others who for years have been offering resistance to the apartheid system and assistance to those who suffer under it.

But the call was not heeded by the state, and the year ended with even more repressive measures: political arrests and censorship of the press. Britain's reaction was typical of world opinion. Sir Geoffrey Howe said: 'Every government has a duty to maintain law and order, but muzzling the press and locking up one's political opponents is not the answer.'

In this gloomy situation, the church is being challenged regarding its traditional belief of the relation of church and state. How it is reacting is the theme of our next chapter.

Chapter Six

The Role of the Church

When I visited Durban on a number of occasions, I was impressed and interested in the Indians and their religion. They were Hindus or Moslems and their temples and central mosque, one of the oldest in Africa, are well worth visiting. They are one of the most important racial groups in the Republic, and exercise an influence which far outweighs their numbers but they, together with those who practise African traditional religion, amount only to 5% of the population, whereas Christians, both black and white, account for about 70%.

But Christians have been divided over the question of apartheid, the white Dutch Reformed Churches arguing for and supporting separate development of the races, and the South African Council of Churches, which we have mentioned in a previous chapter, opposing it. But there is now greater hope of reconciliation between the churches since the Synod of the DRC in 1986 has agreed that apartheid is contrary to the gospel, and has admitted that it has been mistaken.

However, it still remains a mystery to many people why a Christian church could accept such a belief and encourage the state to institute such a development as apartheid. Some see the answer in the Calvinism of the Reformed faith. John Calvin, one of the main reformers in Europe in the sixteenth century, preached a doctrine of predestination, which stressed how God elected a people for salvation.

The settlers, coming to the Cape of Good Hope in 1652, could have come to see this doctrine as indicating that they had been chosen of God to evangelize the natives, and could rightly regard themselves as a race apart. This 'apartness' (apartheid) would be necessary if they were to keep themselves pure to do the work of God and raise the people from their state of paganism. It is to be doubted, however, that the early Dutch settlers were strong Calvinists, and it is now recognized that it was the nineteenth-century experience which laid the groundwork of separate development. The first influence here was the way the Afrikaner viewed his past, especially the experience of the great trek. This exit from the Cape was like the Exodus of the Israelites from Egypt as we noted previously. Like the Israelites of the Old Testament, they too had been chosen by God and led away from the Pharoah (the British) though the land of the Philistines (Blacks) and into the promised land of the Republic. The victory over the Zulus at Blood River and the covenant sealed with God seemed to confirm this divine vocation.

Another influence was the neo-Calvinism of Abraham Kuyper, who was a leading churchman and theologian in Holland in the nineteenth century. He thought that God created and blessed each nation with its own peculiar culture and that this must be preserved. He coined the slogan 'in isolation lies our strength' which meant that Christianity must keep itself pure by separation from those that might defile. Thus emerged a kind of Christian nationalism in the mind of the Afrikaner, and this was very useful to salve a conscience which saw the need for separation between black and white on the more practical grounds of economics and job preservation.[1]

This nationalism was also fuelled in the 1930s and 1940s by German romantic and racist thought which stressed an organic community of soil, blood language, culture, state, tradition, world view, and destiny. Some of the leading architects of apartheid studied in Germany at the time and brought back such ideals to the Fatherland. The most prominent among them was Dr Verwoerd, who was to institute the system in 1948. While only some of the Afrikaners were actual Nazis, these ideas penetrated the minds of many of them and confirmed the view of the church. Thus, it is not surprising to find representatives of the DRC in the 1940s petitioning the government of Smuts and then Malan, with requests for the introducing of a law prohibiting mixed marriages.[2]

Historically, however, the English-speaking churches have opposed separate development, and they, together with the Roman Catholic Church, have sustained the opposition over the years. This opposition has been non-violent and has called for justice and reconciliation between all racial groups. We have seen such opposition taking place in various ways throughout this book. But more recently the influence of North American black theology and Latin American liberation theology has produced articles and books that find fault, not only with the DRC, but also with the English-speaking churches. Thus, in 1985, a powerful document was circulated called *Kairos* (special moment in time) which constituted an attack on the behaviour of the church and on the violence of the state. Unlike other letters, resolutions and confessional documents, *Kairos* is the most radical ever addressed to both church and state in the Republic. It was produced by fifty black ministers working in the townships which have been the scene of riots, burnings and killings during recent times. It has been written at a special time: a national crisis and state of emergency. The document called for signatures indicating support for the view expressed, and hundreds of theologians, pastors and laity have so far put their names to it. It has been translated into a number of languages and stimulated world-wide debate as to the role of the church in such a situation.

Kairos begins with an attack on what it calls state theology. Here, the Dutch Reformed Church is under attack because of its historical support for apartheid. Such theology supports racism, capitalism and totalitarianism, and blesses injustice. It canonizes the will of the powerful, reduces the poor to passivity, and demands obedience and apathy. It uses such scriptural passages as Romans 13.1–7 to give an absolute and divine authority to determine and control the people.

Kairos does not like the passage in Romans because it teaches that the Christian should be submissive to 'the powers that be' i.e. the state, and argues that it was relevant to the situation at Rome but not to the situation in the Republic. Paul, it says, is not writing to a Christian community that is being oppressed by an unjust state, but to those who thought that they could be exonerated from subjection to any kind of political authority. He is not addressing the issue of an unjust state or the need to change one government for another. Hence the passage in Revelation 13 is more relevant to the South African situation since there the state has become the servant of the devil and its days are numbered because God will not permit it to continue. Moreover, the state in the Republic maintains a law and order which is intended to support and endorse the unjust and discriminatory laws of apartheid. Those who refuse to obey the laws of such a state are considered unlawful and disorderly. In these circumstances, Christians cannot accept such laws. The god of the state is an idol who is on the side of the whites who settled in the country and dispossessed the blacks of their land. It is the god of the teargas, rubber bullets, prison cells, and death sentences. Such a god is antichrist. The white Dutch Reformed Church worship and obey such a god. All of this, of course, was written before the DRC renunciation of apartheid, and it will be interesting to see if the black churchmen will revise their opinion of the DRC in the light of this.

Kairos then turns its attack on 'church theology' i.e. the English-speaking churches. These churches stress reconciliation, justice and non-violence. But how can reconciliation be possible between justice and nonjustice, good and evil, God and the devil? The Bible teaches that we are to do away with injustice, evil and the devil, not to try and come to terms with them. There cannot be reconciliation in South Africa today until the present injustices are removed. The state must repent and remove injustices before there can be reconciliation. A theology of direct confrontation is called for rather than reconciliation.

Here, the document emphasizes the biblical teaching that God does not forgive without repentance, and we should not forgive our fellow men until they repent. These views of reconciliation and repentance are debatable, as also is the further point that justice itself is not simply the justice of reform from 'above' (state reforms) but that which comes 'from below' (determined by the people of the country). Church theology, *Kairos* says, addresses appeals to the whites of 'the top of the pile' but such reforms are never a real change. What is needed is a change of structure brought about by the oppressed who stand up for their rights and wage a struggle against their oppressors.

This leads *Kairos* to examine the question of violence. In the black townships, it must be realized that the action of the police and army is violence, not the maintenance of law and order, and the violence of the blacks is the resistance of a defenceless people. There is a long Christian tradition which endorses the use of physical force to defend oneself against aggressors and tyrants. Thus, the document endorses resistance of a violent nature as a last resort against oppression. Further, it castigates church theology for the tacit support it gives to the army by appointing chaplains and not resisting conscription. Such a theology has failed because it is too moralistic and relies on absolute principles which it seeks to apply to every situation.

Hence, the document calls for a prophetic theology. The social situation is that of 'the haves' and the 'have nots'; the oppressor and the oppressed. It demands not reform, but revolution. The Yaweh of the Old Testament is the liberator who does not try to reconcile the Hebrew slaves with their Egyptian oppressors, but to free them: The Jesus of the New Testament comes to proclaim liberty and the freeing of the captives (Ex. 3.79; Luke 4.18–19).

The South African regime is tyrannical and governs in the interests of the white minority only, and in order to maintain its position, it will become more oppressive as resistance to it increases. It must be replaced by a government elected by the majority. While the Christian is called upon to love, he must eliminate oppression wherever he encounters it. How then can the church with its prophetic theology of hope translate words into action? Consumer boycotts and stayaways from work must be supported; church services need to highlight political and social change; consultations, co-ordination, and co-operation must take place with people's organizations actively engaged in the struggle; there should be no co-operation with the tyrannical regime; and prayer for change must go hand in hand with civil disobedience.

We shall offer in the next chapter some comments on this document, but here we note how it reflects black theology in South Africa. Black theology was influenced by the Black Consciousness movements in the States and stresses a black history and culture distinct from the whites. It reflects on the situation in the townships and the struggle for liberation, and tries to think through the central claims of the Christian faith in the light of this experience. One can understand this stress on being black because the official definition had been 'non-whites' which implied that Africans, Indians and coloureds existed only as negative shadows of the whites. It could also mean that the white man thought the 'non-whites' would be satisfied with the shadow of the substance of wealth and power which he took for granted. Writers on black theology see two phases in its development. Phase 1 revolves around the work of Dr Manas Buthelezi, Dr Basil Moore, Dr Allan Boesak and others, and moves from the polemic to the major academic writing of Boesak whose *Farewell to Innocence* (1978) became a text on black theology in seminaries. Then there was a lull followed by phase 2 with which we are principally concerned. This is described in *The Unquestionable Right to be Free* (1986) and was based on two conferences in 1983 and 1984. Contributors were drawn from the universities, adult education centres and the churches.[3]

The striking thing in contrast to previous efforts is the stress on Marxist analysis of the social situation so that class as well as race is seen as part of the problem. This phase of black theology also wants to learn more from the African traditional religions, the African independent churches, black history and the liberation struggle in South Africa as well as what can be gleaned from the African heritage as a whole and from American black theology.

How then do writers of this phase see the relation between black consciousness and black theology? Black consciousness emerged in the late 1960s in the Republic and stressed an attitude of mind or way of life. It contained among other things the following notions: political awareness, pride for 'black is beautiful', concern about culture and liberation.[4] Black theology too is concerned with liberation and tries to show that the Christian gospel supports the advancement of blacks. It thinks about the political implication of the Christian faith in the South African situation and contends for the emancipation of black people from racism.

Black consciousness goes back to Steve Biko the black student leaders of the late 1960s and draws inspiration from his ideas of black identity and political awareness. It coincided with the civil rights movement in the USA and had a relationship with it in terms of ideas and strategy. Further it reacted strongly against the failure of the white Christian church to respond to the political crisis in South Africa. With all of this black theology agrees.

However in the current scene differences have developed. Black consciousness is more sympathetic to the Azanian Peoples organization while black theology has affinity with the United Democratic Front. The first (AZAPO) stresses black solidarity and in that sense is racial while the second (UDF) is non-racial. Another factor is that while black consciousness thinks that race is the problem black theology underlines both race and class. This gives the latter an advantage for it is calling on the 'workers of the world to unite' whatever their colour.

Black theology stresses that salvation is not only spiritual, but has to do with those material things that keep people in slavery and oppression. Sin is a social and political term: 'it describes an oppressive situation, one in which there is no fellowship, no mutual caring for people, and no room to live as a whole human being in freedom and joy.'[5]

Black theology is very conscious of the injustices of the past which have led to the present system. It sees the colonial arrival of Europeans in South Africa as forcing a foreign capitalist system on blacks and relegating them to the position of cheap labourers.[6] This disturbed the natural developments of African socio-economic history, and became a protracted struggle against exploitation and oppression as well as a struggle to regain the land and establish a new social, political and economic system in which the African would be the owner of the means of production and distribution.

The Christian religion aided the development of the present system. It supported in ideological form the social norms of a capitalist civilization and instilled a belief in the virtues of work, private property and respect for authority as well as cultural norms. On the other hand, black theologians recognize that Christianity, because it contains 'the cry of the oppressed creature', can serve as an ideological 'protest against real suffering': this led in the nineteenth century to the moving out of the African Independent churches from the white church.

Black theology surveys the causes of the present unrest in the country and sees this as the culmination of years of detention, economic exploitation, mass trials, poor education, control of the movement of blacks, pass laws, lack of home ownership and meaningful participation in the planning and managing of the black affairs. Some of these have now been reformed and abolished, but resentment lingers on and fuels the fire against the remaining oppressive measures. Thus, since 1984, blacks have killed other blacks, reckoned to be collaborators with the system, and burned and looted public buildings and shops. In their eyes, such property belongs to the system, not to them for they are 'temporary sojourners' in the urban areas.[7] The whole scenario of consumer boycotts, work stoppages, work stayaways, school disruptions, the destruction of selected targets and killing of blacks associated with the apartheid system, is seen by black theology, not as the work of organizations such as the African National Congress, but as the result of the deep-seated discontent of the black masses.

Does then black theology inculcate violence to overthrow the system? This is the big question. It admits that the Christian tradition had tended to uphold 'non-violence', but says that within the very same tradition some speak of 'non-violence as a strategy rather than a principle'. As a strategy, it refuses to retaliate (Matt. 5.38f.) and cites the example of Martin Luther King Jnr. But another Christian tradition says that Christians have a right and even a duty to protect their existence and freedom by proportionate means against an unjust aggressor.

Black theology endorses the use of violence in the sense of resisting a repressive state that has no mandate from the majority of the people. The army and the police represent the whites not the blacks. The church, through the appointment of military chaplains, is seen to give direct moral support and, therefore, approval to the army. Moreover, the church is in an ambivalent situation for both those who kill and those who are killed belong to it. Violence, as thus defined, seems to black theology the only answer because of the state's refusal to negotiate with the ANC and the major Western powers' lack of application of meaningful sanctions against the Republic. The 'just war' concept acknowledges the right of one state to wage war against another but appears not to envisage an unjust aggressor emerging from within the boundaries of a single State.

Black theology is committed to a religion of liberation and it believes that God is a God of justice and requires the liberation of all humanity; it believes that the Bible affirms the ultimate power of the divine majesty over every evil force. Only a Calvinistic interpretation of the will of God (as embraced by the Dutch Reformed Church and more subtly, by other churches in the Republic) could believe that the unequal distribution of the goods of this world was a special dispensation of Divine Providence.

Black theology, grasping the idea of group pride, freedom of the individual, and uniqueness of the black person which it learned from the black consciousness movement goes on to stress the solidarity of the African tradition and preaches 'what belongs to one belongs to all' (In Zulu 'Okwakho okwami').

Life may have to be sacrificed in this just war, but the guerrilla or freedom fighter believes that the God of Israel is on his side and that there is hope for him after death. Revolution as a means of overthrowing an oppressor is based upon the Exodus of the children of Israel from Egypt. It is a last resort since peaceful protest has not changed the mind of the South African government just as the pleading of Moses failed to move the heart of Pharoah.

Thus the picture of God as Liberator from captivity and his condemnation of the injustice done to the poor dominates black theology. God's purpose is to set his people free from bondage and to make all things new. This bondage however extends not only to blacks but also to whites who are corrupted by power and held captive by wealth. Beneath the material prosperity of the whites is the fear of their fate if the system that has favoured them is overthrown. They are bedevilled by anxiety and God wants to set them free. The church, says black theology, has the responsibility of challenging the white man to face the truth of the situation, pacify his fears, and make him want to overthrow the system. Christianity is 'praxis', not theorizing. It is the 'doing of the truth' in a society which has tried to turn the truth of Christianity into a lie. While black theologians are aware of the arguments and debates of theology over the centuries concerning christology, sacraments, salvation, ministerial orders and ecumenicity, they are more interested in ethics and the way the gospel is to be put into practice in their society. I noticed this in the classroom situation. Both black and white students listened with politeness to the arguments of the Fathers and Apologists and Reformers about the Trinity, christology and salvation but when it came to black theology and the theme of liberation the class was charged with an emotion and passion that demonstrated how vital this was to their situation. Arguments about the *Kairos* document and the writing of black theologians were minutely scrutinized and the discussion generated in the classroom went far beyond it. Many of the whites were sympathetic to the views put forward in black theology while others felt that such discussions would only cause dissension and disturb the friendly feeling with their black colleagues. But I felt that it was only by bringing these debatable issues into view that the teaching could become a learning experience for us all and if they were not willing to face these problems what would they do when they were thrust into the parish situation? Thus we persevered with the issues raised: the protest against racism and injustice, cheap reconciliation, the misuse of Christianity to bolster wrong social structures and encourage black subjugation and white domination in the church. In connection with the last point it is sad to reflect that while the Christian church in South Africa has many more blacks than whites in its membership it is whites who hold the ecclesiastical power.

A main problem, however, which detained us for some time was where the starting point should be for theology: the Bible or the existing situation? Some black theologians arguing for the black experience of the situation opt for this as the beginning of their theology and say that the scriptures should be read through the epistemological lenses of the black struggle. Indeed from this viewpoint some of them have become critical of the Bible and believe that there is little sign of revolution in it but an acceptance of the *status quo* and a 'looking for pie in the sky when they die'. Even more stringent is the comment that the Bible 'is a ruling class document and represents the ideological and political interests of the ruling class. Only those engaged in the conflict can observe the kindred struggles of the oppressed and exploited of the biblical communities in the very absence of these struggles in the text.'[8] The *status quo* that Christianity has traditionally supported is capitalism not socialism.

Hence it would appear to some that the ideas of Karl Marx

(1818–83) are more suitable to their situation than any other European philosophy for he maintained that it was action rather than theory that was important. The job of philosophy was not to interpret the world but to change it. While this Marxist tendency departs from black theology in its first phase which did not contemplate joining Christianity with such an ideology it is in line with the revolutionary movement and shows the growing impatience of black theologians with negotiation, discussion and non-violent protest. I think however that this is only true of the more radical members of this group.

There is much in black theology that is in accord with the Christian faith, namely its condemnation of lack of brotherhood, inequalities, the disturbance of family life, the inferior form of education, the creation of division among the races and the refusal to give everyone the chance of sharing in the material wealth of the country . . . but tendencies to side with the way of revolution to overthrow the system do not correspond with the Christian gospel. This is indeed recognized, as we have noted, by those who admit that this way of bringing about change is difficult to find in the Bible.

Still the image of God as liberator is surely correct and I think they have made a good case for this liberation to be both material and spiritual for the brotherhood inspired by conversion leads to an attempt to establish equality in society. If the kingdom of God is socialistic then this theology is a corrective of the church which forgets the social gospel and rests content with the development of the inner spiritual life. Further, it is right in seeing oppression applying not only to the poor but also to the rich since the story of Jesus' encounter with the rich young ruler (Luke 18.18ff.) indicates that liberation for him was more difficult than for the poor masses. But God is not only liberator he is also Father, reconciler, forgiver, shepherd etc. and these images convey the impression that God tries to persuade, reason, forgive and seek the sinner. Even negotiation is not ruled out! Hence our idea of God must be a balanced one and not a concentration on an image which might give the impression that revolution is justified. And as Christians, while respecting the Old Testament as the root of our faith, we must put stress on New Testament teaching and the development of non-violent resistance. This we will explore later. Again, black theology concentrates on that prophetic tradition where the prophets in Israel were outside the ecclesiastical and political circle. This is a correct emphasis for it shows how God condemns injustice but it does not rule out those who are within the system and protest vigorously when injustice occurs. Nathan the prophet, for example, who was within the system did not hesitate to condemn David for his affair with Bathsheba (II Sam. 12).

Then there is the question of the starting point for theology: the Bible or the situation. Jesus as is well known not only used illustrations and material drawn from real life situations but addressed his message to the poor, the captive, the blind, the rich and the powerful. Can such a message be relevant to conflict situations in our day? Some scholars argue that there is a radical discontinuity between the world of the New Testament and ours. I have tried to deal with this point elsewhere[9] and cannot go into detail about it here but simply note that the difference appears to be in degree rather than in kind: the culture gap is not as wide as some would assert and there is a common element in human beings which spans the time gap.

However, black theology at times comes from a situation which seems to demand a revolutionary type of action and tries to find confirmation for this action in scripture. Sometimes black theologians find what they want to find but, as we have seen, it can happen that they confess to its absence. Is the right way not to try and listen to what the scripture says rather than project our proposed plan of action upon it? We may not like to hear what it says but can we disobey the message? For some of course there is an alternative way and this has been embraced by liberation theology in Latin America and is now seen to be influencing black theology in South Africa: the way of Karl Marx.

For some Christians of course the mention of Marx or Communism is anathema! Such an ideology is condemned without a hearing but this is not possible when we are searchers after truth. What Marx wrote about the condition of the poor and the need for justice should have been preached by the church in nineteenth-century England and if it had been, the working classes might have been retained by the churches. As it is many churches in England nowadays continue to exist financially on the bequests of past members and a membership of the middle classes, hence black theology is right in openly exposing the injustice of the situation so that the church will not share the same fate in South Africa. Again, there are various forms of Marxism, and Marx himself was not a militant atheist as were the leaders of Communism such as Lenin and Stalin. They developed an elitist party which they considered was necessary to rule the proletariat and went against what Marx called the dictatorship of the people. Marx stressed the arousing of the people to their true interests and did not appear to hold that the party should rule over them. It is true that the early Marx did speak of a violent overthrow but later he did not rule out gradual structural reform and even peaceful revolution. Since Marx was a socialist before he became an atheist there is no reason why socialism should necessarily be atheistic. Only if religion allows itself to be an instrument in the hands of the ruling class can it be an obstacle to change. Certainly both Christianity and Communism contend for the hungry, the thirsty, the naked, the stranger and the prisoner. The Christian God revealed in Jesus Christ calls for the healing of all human life and that must mean the economic structure of our day which accounts for many of these ills. Perhaps there is in Marxism 'signals of transcendence' that not only judge the church but enable it to contribute to a better world. However, can one embrace certain characteristics of Marxism without going all the way? If, as some of these theologians say, the Bible is a 'middle-class' document and that there is little indication of revolution in it, then is Marxism not the answer? And does the ANC not tend towards that position? But to embrace Marx totally means the end of religion for according to him religion arises not because of God but out of the social and economic conditions. Once these deplorable conditions are removed in the new Utopia, religion will disappear. Of course some argue that religion will still have an entry point because of the mystery surrounding suffering, pain and death. These will be alienating factors in this kingdom of man upon the earth. Existing communistic states hardly indicate that sin has disappeared!

But how to inject Christian values and the idea of God into such a society which has attained its Utopia by violence is difficult to see. Man will view it as his work divorced from God (unlike the Exodus) and is likely to have no need of 'that hypothesis' or the virtues of humility, long-suffering, patience, meekness (slave morality according to Neitzsche) inculcated by Christianity. Such a revolution has succeeded by virtue of physical strength and good fire power and it is difficult to understand how violent men can build their kingdom on 'spiritual power'. Nor is there any guarantee that history is going to be proved wrong when it teaches that the oppressed of today when they gain power become the oppressor of tomorrow. The Afrikaner was oppressed by the English and had to make his Exodus from the Cape Colony. He eventually became a guerrilla fighter against continued British oppression but once power came into his hands he became unjust and oppressive against the blacks. The oppressed became the oppressor and the Afrikaner, having learned this from his own past, fears that black majority rule in South Africa will follow the same pattern.

We shall discuss the problem of violence later and the role of the church as the suffering mediator and active participator in non-violent resistance, but in concluding this chapter we note that black theology is presenting a major challenge to the main line churches in South Africa and is calling them to define more clearly their role in this strife-torn country. Sometimes it verges to the extreme left in its understanding of the relation of church and state, not only arguing that the church must be involved in politics but play a role in the revolutionary movements. At the opposite end is the view of church and state embraced by the

Nationalist Party and crystallized in the words of the Prime Minister: 'I see the state and church as two independent bodies both of whom are appointed by God, each with its own commission, task and field. For this reason the state does not want to meddle in the affairs of the church and does not expect the church to meddle in the affairs of the state' (P. W. Botha, 1980). Again in 1984, Botha made his position clear in replying to a letter from the General Secretary of the South African Council of Churches which requested him to meet with their member churches: 'When evidence becomes available that the churches comprising the SACC relinquish political terrain and revert to spiritual matters, then, and not before, will I and members of my cabinet be prepared to meet the leaders concerned.' Moreover, Botha insists that the Fatherland and its defence must be put before the individual conscience. Thus, in 1970, he refused the right of religion to support conscientious objection to military service: 'The honour and duty to defend one's country should not be made subservient to one's religious convictions.'

Both left and right views of the relation of church and state have been reflected in the history of the church. The point of view that church and state are independent and separate (though we have seen that the DRC has exercised quite an influence on the state and still does) stands in stark contrast to the other views which have operated at different times in the past, namely, that the state has the right to rule over the church or conversely that the church has the right to rule over the state.

Botha's view was conveyed very vividly in a TV programme concerned with liberation theology which I saw one evening. In defence of such a position various American evangelists and preachers were interviewed who, from a fundamentalist position, argued that the gospel was concerned with individual spiritual conversion and had no direct concern with social and political issues. But for the church to take up this position would be to side with the Lutheranism in Germany that refused to criticize Hitler and the clear injustice of his movement. Such views of the relation of church and state are still heard in England. Hence the Bishop of Durham was criticized in recent times for daring to interfere with the miners' strike and attacking the changes in the welfare services. This kind of criticism goes far back in time and was well stated by that master of economics Adam Smith (1723-1790) when he asserted that economic laws exclude Christian moral considerations. Even more vivid was Hitler's declaration to Pastor Martin Niemoller whom he later imprisoned: 'You confine yourself to the church. I'll take care of the German people.'

For the Christian, however, who believes in the universality and lordship of Christ, there can be no separation between his spiritual and inward life and the outward practice. His faith will produce good works. Hence if he is a politician his ideas of justice will be governed by Christian principles and moral considerations. If this had been practised by politicians in South Africa and economics not made the first consideration, the condition of the black population would not be what it is there today even if the right to vote had not been given to them. It is remarkable that a state which declares itself to be Christian gives priority to economics and then condemns Communism which itself maintains, following Marx, that economics is the determining factor in history!

Whatever we may say about Communism, and one can be very critical of it, there is the attempt to lift the working conditions and standards of the poor and this is a Christian emphasis. This Marxist influence we have noted both in the view of the ANC and black theology. The need is for the churches in the Republic to embrace this socialistic aspect of the gospel without becoming Marxists for if they do not their ultimate history could be that of the church in Russia. Ironically, the state in Russia forbids the church to meddle in politics and thus resembles the position of the state in South Africa which says that it is opposed to Communism!

In conclusion we would stress that the church in the New Testament is opposed to violent revolution but that does not mean that the church must always obey the state. When such disobedience might occur, however, is the debatable question. Should for example it take place when the state calls upon the Christian to fight an unjust war or a war against the will of God? The difficulty here is how we are to know what God's will is and when a war is just or unjust. Was the Falkland's war a just one? The answer will differ depending on what nationality we are but there is also some evidence that Christians in Britain had their doubts.

Again, it may be asked if such disobedience to the state means that in circumstances of injustice and oppression the Christian has the right to overthrow rulers by force. We need to examine this in the light of the just war concept and the involvement of the Christian in acts of civil disobedience. To this we now turn.

Chapter Seven

Violence or Non-Violence?

Two matters emerged in the last chapter which I discovered are to the fore in any discussion concerning change in South Africa: violence and the just war concept.

Violence in a nuclear age between the superpowers is ruled out of course and the advocates of non-violence have won the day, for it is either non-violence or non-existence. There are rumours that South Africa has tested an atomic bomb and if this is so they might consider using it if they found themselves with their backs against the wall, but let us assume it is just a rumour and think of violence in terms of traditional weapons.

Pacifists in general hold the doctrine of no violent resistance in any circumstances, even in self-defence. They refuse to cooperate with any form of warfare: all disputes must be settled by negotiation. For Christian pacifists a significant text is the sermon on the mount (Matt. 5-7) and some have taken this in a literal fashion, but most commentators argue that it illustrates in various ways how the love of God works and endorses the principle that evil must be overcome with good.

What we will be contending for in this chapter is active resistance of a peaceful nature based on evidence from the New Testament and then going on to consider the just war concept and modern attempts to practise non-violent resistance in conflict situations.

First of all, there is a pattern of thought both in the teaching of

Jesus, and in the epistles which enjoins co-operation with the state and obedience to it. Stories about a person reflect what he is like and there is the famous question put to Jesus about the giving of tribute to Caesar and the answer that the disciples should pay it (Mark 12.13ff. and parallels). Something was due to Caesar and something was due to God. We shall take up this obedience to God later but I want to note here that the stories of the temptation of Jesus make clear that he renounced any thought of setting up a worldly state or the use of force to prevent his death on the cross (Matt. 26.51-56). Further, when they wanted to make him a king, he refused.

Consequently Jesus opposed bringing in the kingdom by worldly methods of force. Even the title of Messiah was rejected by him because of its political overtones (Mark 8.29; 15.2; Luke 22.67f.; John 18.33ff.). The state, for him, was not a divine institution, but he accepted it and did not attempt to overthrow it. Persecution, distress, imprisonment will happen to the Christian but there is no indication that he is to resist (Matt. 10.17-23). He receives tax collectors who collaborate with the state and dines with them and accepts one of them into discipleship. He refuses violence for this is the way states are often inaugurated and teaches that he that takes the sword shall perish by the sword (Matt. 26.52, cf. Rev. 13.10 and 22.11).

In such a revolutionary climate as first-century Palestine this message was not liked by the Zealot and was misunderstood by the Romans. The latter condemned him as a rebel; 'King of the Jews' was the inscription on the cross which meant a rebel against Rome. The disciples at times carried swords, one of them was a Zealot, and Jesus had to say to them that his kingdom was a different one from that which they conceived. It is argued by some that Judas may have been a Zealot whose betrayal was to force Jesus into a position where he would have to use his power in order to escape death.

There is another theme that runs through the gospels: suffering. Jesus must suffer and the disciples will suffer. Jesus comes to reveal not a God of worldly power and pomp but a God who suffers, in his Son, the death on the cross. The words and story of the Last Supper enshrine this teaching (Mark 8.27ff.; 9.30–32; 10.32–34; 12.1–12, and the passion narrative, cf. parallels in other Gospels). The suffering will not only bring salvation to men but draw them to Christ: 'I, if I be lifted, up will draw all men unto me' (John 12.32).

Thus it is not by force or violence that the kingdom of God will be established in the hearts of men. They will not be compelled by force but drawn by suffering love.

We could take examples of this from history but in modern times it was quite remarkable how people all over the world were moved by the suffering of children in Nigeria during the civil war, and more recently the suffering in the black townships in South Africa. On the other hand they condemned violence on the part of white against black, black against white, and black against black. The structure of the South Africa government was put under tremendous external pressure by the power of suffering.

In the epistles, the same theme is sounded: obedience to the state and the suffering of love (Rom. 13.1f.; I Peter 2.13f.; I Tim. 2.1f.; Titus 3.1f.; Cor. 13). This suffering is necessary even if its cause is unjust and oppressive. I Peter in particular points to the example of Christ: 'He committed no sin, he was convicted of no falsehood; when he was abused he did not retort with abuse, when he suffered he uttered no threats, but committed his cause to the One who judges justly' (I Peter 3.22–23).

The state, according to Paul, judges and distinguishes between good and evil, and punishes the evil. But I Peter questions whether the authorities can distinguish properly between good and evil (Pilate was unable to do so when he charged Jesus with being a rebel) and yet the Christian is still required to suffer and not take revenge. He must pray for the state. This is quite remarkable in that the Roman state was heathen, and was compared to the beast in the book of Revelation (Rev. 13). The state was demanding worship and was 'an abomination' since it was putting itself in the place of God (Mark 13).

We know from sources outside the New Testament, that Christians were called upon to worship the image of the emperor (Pliny to Trajan *c.* AD 115). Further, we know that the suffering endured for the refusal to do this by the Christians excited even the pity of the merciless Romans. (Tacitus, *Annales* xv. 44, *c.* AD 64).

The Christian, as Jesus said, gives Caesar his due, i.e. obedience, taxes etc., but also obeys God. When the state demands worship, the Christian resists, but even here, he does not seek to overthrow it. He rather puts it to shame by his suffering. This again is remarkable when we consider that the book of Revelation has as its background the terrible persecution of the church by Rome. When Caesar demanded what was rightly due to God alone then the Christian was required to obey God rather than men. In so doing, the state has yielded to the demonic, and instead of keeping order and preventing chaos, it worships the demons of this world (Matt. 4.8f.; Luke 4.6; John 18.36). Power corrupts and absolute power absolutely corrupts. Such a state will be brought to an end by God (Rev. 13.14ff., cf. Acts 12.19ff.).

Now there can be little doubt that many Jews grew impatient with this suffering and obedience to an unjust state. It was so then, it is so now. The Maccabeans and the Zealots demanded and tried a holy war but the taking up of worldly weapons availed them nothing while the church of the New Testament conquered the Roman world by its love, compassion, and suffering.

With this positive statement relating church and state we now turn to how the *Kairos* document uses scripture. As we have mentioned the writers see a contradiction between passages such as Romans 13.1–7 and other verses in the Bible where God does not demand obedience to oppressive leaders.

The standard argument against this viewpoint is that as far as the New Testament is concerned obedience is required except when the state is demanding worship. This is correct according to

VIOLENCE OR NON-VIOLENCE?

our exegesis of Paul's instructions in Romans 13.1-7. When we give the political power its due then this is the outworking of love. Also we have drawn attention to other passages in the New Testament which far from contradicting the passage in Romans, confirm it.

We must then consider the other passages which *Kairos* draws attention to, namely Revelation 13. Here we agree with the document that the state is demonic for it demands the worship which can only rightly be given to God. In the context it is Rome that is referred to but Rome is only the current embodiment of evil and it could be any state before or after.

So far, we have noted the theme of non-resistance; does Revelation 13 continue this and underline the teaching of Jesus that 'all who take the sword die by the sword?' Yes, it does, even though the sufferings of the Christians under the persecution are severe. In particular, verse 10 stresses the teaching of Jesus: 'Whoever kills with the sword must with the sword be killed.' They must suffer as Christ has suffered and thus win the victory.

When the resistance to the Roman rule occurred in Palestine, the result was the destruction of Jerusalem. Instead of this madness, the Christians in the book of Revelation are called upon in this very chapter 13 which is cited by the *Kairos* document to endure: 'This calls for the endurance and faith of God's people', not the taking up of the sword against Rome (v. 10).

It is God who determines the beginning and end of the Beast and it is God who will bring its power and dominion to an end. The Christians were called upon to worship the Beast, i.e. the state as represented by the emperor. If they did not worship, they were killed. It was usual for everyone to take part in this emperor cult and a mark was placed upon the forehead of those who complied. This mark was necessary even for the purpose of carrying on business in the market place since those who did not possess it were not traded with. Thus, this chapter of Revelation does not give support to violence, even if we define it as resistance against evil as the *Kairos* document maintains.

We must now discuss the question of reconciliation, and our first question as raised by the document is: Who takes the initiative in reconciliation?

When we turn to the New Testament, the whole theme is that God takes the initiative in reconciliation. It is the story of God's search for man summarized in the Pauline statement, 'God was in Christ reconciling the world unto himself (II Cor. 5.19). The movement of Jesus among scribes, Pharisees, tax collectors, prostitutes and Zealots, was the reaching out of God to save. God did not demand the world to turn in repentance to him before he came, indeed his initiative was to cause men to turn to him in repentance. Should the church in South Africa not call upon all to repent, for who is the Pharisee who says that he does not need such repentance? If leading churchmen write letters to the government asking them to negotiate with the ANC, then they must also write letters to the ANC calling upon them to negotiate. Who will do the Christian thing first and put aside the weapons so that peaceful negotiations may begin?

In other words, the church puts both state and 'freedom fighters' to the test to see who is Christian. If the state refuses to negotiate when arms are laid down, then world opinion and Christianity will condemn it. The past years have shown that the Republic cannot ignore world opinion for it ultimately involves the economic factor which is the 'Achilles heel' of any state.

The Bible speaks quite clearly of the reconciliation of the world and stresses that we love our enemies. Jesus is the mediator between God and man and by his death and resurrection he has brought reconciliation. Should not the church also mediate between opposing parties and try to bring about reconciliation? In so doing, it will need to criticize the methods and thinking of both.

We now return to the question of obedience to the state. So far the exposition has revealed passive aspects but we need to go deeper into the meaning of the Greek word translated 'obedience'. It does not always mean 'to obey' but is used of a reciprocal obliga-

VIOLENCE OR NON-VIOLENCE?

tion between Christians (Eph. 5.21) and while 'subjecting yourselves one to another in the fear of Christ' means recognizing the claims of the other before self it does not mean a cringing obedience. Passages then such as Rom. 13.1; I Peter 2.13f.; Titus 3.1, while demanding obedience and responsible conduct under the rule of the state do not require an uncritical adherence to every command.[1]

This position is confirmed by the limits to what is owed to Caesar (Mark 12.17), the criticizm of a ruler such as Herod Antipas, 'that fox' (Luke 13.32), and Paul's rebuke of the magistrates of Philippi (Acts 16.35ff.). Paul refused to depart meekly from their city and insisted that they come in person to release him and Silas. John the Baptist too came into conflict with Herod and did not hesitate to rebuke him for his manner of life (Mark 6.18; Luke 3.19). In fact when we consider the opening chapters of the Acts of the Apostles there is continual conflict between the disciples and the religious and political authorities which usually ended in the former being imprisoned and sometimes beaten. According to the record the disciples were being disobedient in witnessing to God's revelation in Jesus and proclaiming his death and resurrection as the way of salvation for all men. They accused the authorities of being against Jesus from the beginning (Acts 4.26) and stated that both Herod and Pontius Pilate were part of the opposition. In reply the Jewish religious leaders demanded the imprisonment of the disciples as often as they could.

It is significant to see what the apostles accused the authorities of doing. They had denied the truth and committed murder in bringing about the death of Jesus. Their preference was for a murderer rather than the holy and just one (Acts 2.23; 3.14). The apostles opposed such injustice and called for a community characterized by brotherhood, equality, and the sharing of goods (Acts 2.44f.; 4.34–37). All forms of discrimination whether of wealth or race of religion were to be abolished (Col. 3.11). These were the principles accepted in the early church and when the disciples were told to be silent they replied: 'We must obey God rather than men' (Acts 5.29). In pursuit of these beliefs they did not use violence but violence of all kinds was used against them. Since, as we have seen, the South African state has over the years acted contrary to these principles, the church there has the right to protest, criticize and disobey whenever these have been infringed but there does not seem to be any ground for armed rebellion. As for the important point which has troubled many Christians in the Republic – military service on behalf of the state – there is no direct answer. Jews were exempt from military service and since the Romans had plenty of volunteers they did not need to conscript. To base actions on the implicit teaching of scripture is risky but the Christian could argue that since the state has the right to use force (Rom. 13.4) and is divinely ordained and the cause was just and undertaken in the last resort then he could serve in the army.[2] This gives ground for the just war idea which we shall examine shortly.

But some commentators also see the possibility of armed rebellion. They point out that Jesus was opposed to the Zealots but this does not mean that in all circumstances he would have been against armed resistance. Perhaps it might be argued that he opposed rebellion since in general the Roman state was not unjust or that he knew that it had no chance of success. Against these conjectures we can say that he ruled out force as the way of achieving his goal and the bringing in of the kingdom of God and this kingdom was of a different kind from the one accomplished by men of violence.

It seems certain that in the history of the first three hundred years of the Christian church Christians did not participate in warfare, though Tertullian in the second century does refer to Christians being in the army. This can be interpreted as referring to soldiers who had been converted to the faith. After the acceptance of Christianity as the main religion of the Roman Empire with the conversion of Constantine, Christians as part of their duty to the state did serve in the army but clergy were exempt and it was not until Augustine (350–430) that the just war concept emerged.

VIOLENCE OR NON-VIOLENCE?

In his teaching a just war was to be conducted by the laity in the cause of justice and to bring conflict to an end. The church's thinking beyond Augustine carefully limited killing to combatants and excluded attacks on civilians or churches, but the Crusades involved the leadership of Christian armies by bishops: offensive as well as defensive war was allowed, and the idea of vengeance against infidels and heretics became acceptable. Indeed the Christian soldier who participated in such wars was assured of eternal salvation if he died in battle.

During the mediaeval period, the Reformation, and in modern times, certain conditions developed with regard to this just war concept and it might be helpful to state these and then see how armed resistance in South Africa could be viewed from this standpoint:

1. The war must be declared by a legitimate authority.
2. It must be fought for a just cause and goal.
3. It must be undertaken as a last resort.
4. The conflict must be fought by moderate means.
5. There must be a reasonable chance of success.
6. There needs to be a moral certainty that justice will win.
7. Respect should be shown to neutrals and the Christian community.

With regard to the first condition the ANC would argue that they have legitimate authority, for the majority of the people would vote for them in an election. Their political front is the UDF and this claim I think is correct.

The second principle could also be accepted since the ANC is fighting for equality, brotherhood, and justice for all. Of course whether or not minorities would receive just treatment in the event of their victory would remain to be seen.

The third condition is debatable and I do not think that a last resort has been reached for there is evidence of a reforming process and imprisoned leaders of the ANC have been released. There is still hope that Nelson Mandela will also be released soon.

Moderate means is being used in the conflict and the ANC has not gone to the extent of some Western nations during the last two World Wars. How would America be judged in the light of this principle in using the atomic bomb against the Japanese?

How far can the ANC succeed? I am inclined to the opinion that there would need to be both an external and internal attack to guarantee any hope of success. And one of the drawbacks to an internal insurrection is the fact that the ANC does not have Zulu support.

With regard to moral certainty, the ANC believe that they are fighting for justice and this will sustain their morale in the arduous struggle. Respect for the rights of neutrals has not been adhered to and we have noted the embarrassment of Oliver Tambo when he was questioned about bombings in which innocent civilians, both black and white, were killed. Of course both Britain and America in fighting the last World War said that the cause was just but failed in this respect so the ANC could argue that 'people who live in glass houses should not throw stones'.

In general then from the Christian perspective the ANC is not straying too far from the principles that govern a just war, but the debate continues on the important point of whether the situation is a last resort or whether it might be possible to negotiate a settlement peacefully.

In the history of the church it is interesting to note that at the time of the Reformation only the Anabaptists and the Quakers held to what they considered to be the pacifism of the New Testament while the main Reformation churches embraced the just war idea. This has been continued up to the present day and it might be useful to take an example of a modern and eminent theologian in the Reformed tradition, Karl Barth, who experienced a situation of tyranny and injustice and was involved in the church's struggle against Hitler. Barth deals with such questions in his monumental *Church Dogmatics*, but he is even more direct in *Table Talk* with students.

When he was asked what criteria there were for the overthrow of an unjust government he gave three:

VIOLENCE OR NON-VIOLENCE?

1. A government may be overthrown if it shows injustice to such an extent that the point is reached where you have the conviction that it can no longer continue to exist but we must be sure of this: 'Perhaps it is wise to wait a little. If you are sure (before God) that the government is intolerable then you may think of revolution but perhaps not attempt it.'[3]

2. We must be sure that it is the last resort.

3. 'If you are sure revolution must come then you must still ask yourself this question; have you a real opportunity to better the situation? Revolution is not so difficult but what will you do the next day? If you are not sure that good can come of it then do not do it. There have been too many revolutions in which the first and second conditions have been met but not the third. This was my reservation about the plot to overthrow Hitler. Bonhoeffer and his friends were not clear about what would happen afterwards... There was not a clear positive position. Negative, yes. But clear vision on practical possibilities was lacking. They were dreamers. No, if you are sure on all three points then you must pray and ask God if He is also of the same mind... here we are back to the absolute criterion.'[4]

Concerning the commandment: 'Thou shalt not kill', Barth translates more correctly 'Thou shalt not murder' and points out that in the Old Testament there were killings for God's sake. A soldier has to do this and Barth taking his stand on the principle of the last resort leaves open the possibility of war. He himself joined the army to protect Switzerland from the Nazis and he had to guard a bridge over the Rhine which separated the two countries. He commented: 'If one of my Christian friends in Germany had tried to blow up the bridge I would have had to shoot.'[5]

I think that Barth's third point is important for the South African situation since, though the ANC charter has a programme to follow after majority rule, it is not clear that it is acceptable to the population as a whole. The middle-class black fears such a socialist programme and since the Zulus oppose the ANC the country could experience a civil war.

However let us now pursue the more excellent way of suffering love (I Cor. 13) which has emerged as one of the themes of the New Testament and use it as a *via media* between absolute withdrawal and the just war concept. This is called: non-violent resistance and was developed by Mahatma Gandhi. Using insights from both Hinduism and Christianity he tried the technique of non-violent resistance in South Africa and India. During his time in the Republic he got the state to repeal legislation aimed at the Indian community and prevented the Indians from being hounded out of the country, and on his return to India he was instrumental in winning independence from the British (14 August 1947). Martin Luther King Jr in America employed the same technique of non-violence to break down racial barriers and pave the way for the civil rights Act of 1968.

The following summarizes the method:

1. Gandhi used the word, 'satyagrapha' meaning courage, selflessness, compassion and a firm stand for justice. It was based on the Sermon on the Mount which taught the overcoming of evil with good and involved suffering by refusing the act of reprisal when injured and seeking to love the one who caused it. Martin Luther King followed the same pathway. On the 30 January 1956 his house was dynamited, yet standing amid the ruins he said: 'We believe in law and order. Don't get panicky. Don't do anything at all. Don't get out your weapons. He who lives by the sword will perish by the sword. Remember that is what God said. We are not advocating violence. We want to love our enemies. We must love our white brothers no matter what they do to us.'[6]

In connection with the trouble in South Africa Kenneth Kaunda, who achieved Zambia's independence by non-violence, contends that if white Christians there were committed to suffering to dismantle apartheid the state would take more notice. On the other hand, the suffering of blacks is unheeded because it is commonplace. It is true of course that some white Christians have suffered in the Republic but it has not been general. However if it became so using the technique of non-violence, it would unite black and white not only in the struggle but for the better order when victory is achieved.[7]

2. Non-violent resistance must be carefully planned and executed. There is the right time, place and object. The breaking of laws, demonstrations, protests, strikes, boycotts, with the resulting imprisonment, beatings, and even risk of death, must be so timed that they will have the maximum effect on world opinion and be recorded by the media. This requires discipline and reasonableness in the face of unreasonable violence in order to shame the forces of the state and the moderate who stresses order rather than justice.

Such massive resistance in South Africa could bring the economic life of the country to a standstill. But leaders would need to be trained and as they were arrested in the protest movement replaced by others. Of course the selection of a certain object is important and so is full concentration on it. Thus in Montgomery, USA, the object was the boycott of buses and this was organized with great efficiency. A car pool was established and maintained over a period of twelve months and blacks who owned cars transported poorer blacks to their jobs and drove others to shops etc. Taxis were used and a programme of education in discipline and morale instituted to prevent feelings of violence arising when the situation became difficult. Eventually a panel of judges in May 1956 declared that the segregation of buses in Montgomery was unconstitutional and the Supreme Court order swiftly followed.[8]

While I was in South Africa blacks did try to boycott white shops at different times but it was poorly organized, did not have the support of the whites, and many blacks were disgusted to find that black traders in the townships were pricing the food higher than the white shops. Greed apparently had triumphed over the justice of the cause.

3. Self-defence is permissible. Martin Luther King said that the blacks had the right to defend themselves when attacked but it would be non-violence that would expose the injustices and Gandhi would have argued that there are particular circumstances

that called for self-defence and he encouraged his people to enlist as medical orderlies in war. He believed in an armed force for the maintaining of order but he saw its role as co-operating with the citizens and he hoped that the day would come when armies would be obsolete.[9] When the just cause operates it is in order to serve in the forces as non-combatants. There may be, however, some inconsistency here, i.e. to believe in self-defence and restriction to non-combatant activity at one and the same time.

There are other elements in non-violent resistance which we cannot go into here but in concluding this chapter we consider some criticisms which might be directed against its use in South Africa. It could be argued that Gandhi was dealing with the British and they have a traditional sense of justice and fair play and Martin Luther King was operating in a democracy, but the Republic is a totalitarian regime where elections that count are confined to the small white minority.

This is true but in reply we would point out that the state in the New Testament was totalitarian and yet the Christians who appeared to be basically pacifists not only successfully endured violence but emerged to become the principal religion of the empire. Various reasons have been put forward as to why this happened and the conversion of Constantine heads the list, but it also must have been connected with their impressive way of life which contained elements of the satyagrapha mentioned above.

Concerning the British sense of fair play, one likes to think that this has been so over the years but dealings with the Afrikaner in the Boer war, especially in connection with the concentration camps, does not reflect this. The world rightly condemns apartheid but it was created and maintained on the basis of fear. Only a united effort on the part of both black and white will remove the system and the fear that goes with it.

Many black Christians recognize that the small white minority needs reassurance as to what would happen to them under majority rule and non-violent measures to bring about change are more likely to convince them of their future security than violent, for how can they believe that men who have overcome them by violence will not further extend that force once they come to power? Co-operation by black and white in bringing about change by non-violent means would pave the way for further co-operation in some form of power-sharing as a short term goal and majority rule in the long term. If black and white suffer now for a change of dispensation then in the new rule there is much greater hope of peace and justice. This is more than an ideal, for the majority of people in the Republic are Christians and the DRC is now united with the others against the apartheid system. What is needed is to put the principles of Christian non-violent resistance into operation.

Of course, it must be admitted that this requires world-wide media coverage and Pretoria has been quick to clamp down here when it saw the amount of damage done to its reputation during 1984 and 1985. Hence the hard censorship of today. However, impatience is one of the cause of armed rebellion and one can detect that in the Republic, but it is salutary to note that in one of the most democratic and fully-developed countries of the world, the USA, it is only about twenty years ago that the civil rights movement had to suffer to enable blacks to use their vote fully and bring about desegregation and equal opportunity. It is true, unlike South Africa, that the blacks had the vote but they were often prevented from using it by barriers that various states had erected. Britain, for her part, is the mother of democracy, yet it has an apartheid situation on its doorstep: Ulster. There is no legalized apartheid as in the Republic but the results of Ulster Protestant rule over the years yielded similar effects: separate housing, education, social life. Again it is only a little over twenty years ago that the civil rights movement there was marching in opposition to the injustice that operated in local elections which prevented Catholics getting the majority of council seats in cities such as Londonderry. We who grow impatient with the slow process of change in South Africa should recognize that problems that are far away seem to us easier to solve than those at home. It is true that South Africa is much better developed than other African countries, but compared to Britain and America it needs time to progress both politically and socially.[10]

Of significance for those wanting change in the Republic is the experience of the civil rights movement in America, where the same choice of what means to be used had to be faced. Was it to be violence as represented by Malcolm X or non-violence as represented by Martin Luther King Jr: black power or black peaceful non-resistance? Malcolm X was convinced that the whole political system must be destroyed, just as many argue today in South Africa. He was fiercely critical of King and called him 'the best weapon that the white man ... has ever gotten in this country'[11] and he together with militant leader Stokely Carmichael wanted whites to be excluded from civil rights marches. King countered not only on the principle of non-violence but on the common sense insight that violent confrontation required resources that they did not have and would only give the police the excuse to wipe out scores of blacks.[12] He feared too that this racial prejudice which had developed among militant blacks would prevent change and become very ominous for the future. His object was a just and united multi-racial community. Finally, we mention a point made by that elder statesman in Africa affairs: Kenneth Kaunda. He is somewhat pessimistic about change in South Africa without violence, but he has spent much time thinking about the method of non-violence. He sees the two as complementary in the sense that non-violence is most effective against a background of violence because the state under pressure will choose to negotiate with the non-violent. No doubt there are problems about this argument but if taken seriously then the way is open for Christians in South Africa to engage in a campaign of non-violent resistance against the background of what the ANC is doing.

In any case Christians there need to think carefully about such a method of achieving change if their churches are going to retain their influence in the new dispensation which cannot be that far away.

Chapter Eight

What of the Future?

Recent events in South Africa demonstrate that delicate balance between hope and despair that we have seen throughout this book. Since many commentators occupy themselves solely with the latter element we begin this chapter looking for signs of hope.

In January 1987 one of the major forces on the scene, the ANC, showed a certain willingness to negotiate. Mr Oliver Tambo's speech in the Zambian capital of Lusaka was characterized by a conciliatory tone as he called upon the whites to join the struggle against apartheid. He called for the building of a new country through the partnership of the races and declared that his organization had been willing to enter into negotiations when the Eminent Persons Group had visited the country, but Pretoria had rejected such overtures and had sent a strike force against their bases. This conciliatory tone attracted world-wide attention at the time and confirms what we had noted in our examination of the ANC beliefs in an earlier chapter.

Then the state announced that prisoners could be released without the proviso of renouncing violence and this led to the freedom of ANC leader, Govan Mbeki. Since he is a close associate of Nelson Mandela and had been in jail with him on Robben Island, speculation became rife that Mandela himself would be released.

Again, after the elections of 1987 Botha announced at the new opening of parliament that he would be taking a more direct role in negotiations with black leaders and followed this statement with advertisements in the media appealing to those leaders to come forward. His new negotiator, Dr Stoffel van der Merwe, said that he was willing to talk to 'radicals' even if they were in jail or detention.

Then there was the very surprising event of the giving of the freedom and honorary citizenship of the black townships of Sharpville, Sebokeng and four others (about 400,000 people) to P. W. Botha in June of 1987. This was startling since the remembrance of Sharpville in particular, where sixty-nine demonstrators had been gunned down by the police, had always strengthened the revolutionary struggle. But here was Botha being received by massed crowds and called the 'great leader' by the mayor.

This was followed by the curious affair recorded by the newspaper in Soweto. During the May elections it carried out a poll to try and discover who its black leaders would elect if given the chance. Among the names that figured in the top twenty alongside Nelson and Winnie Mandela, Desmond Tutu, Oliver Tambo and Allan Boesak was P. W. Botha.

How are we to interpret these last two events? Some would explain the reception of Botha by the black townships as the work of the 'puppet' councillors which he has installed there, but if so how did they convince the people to support it? Again, how did they dare to do it in view of the punishment handed out to councillors who have been 'necklaced' (burning tyre around the neck) and which has been seen world wide on TV? How is the voting in Soweto to be explained? The editor of the newspaper expressed amazement at the results. Without placing much reliance on either event perhaps we might see reflected – what I certainly experienced during my time in the country – quite a good spirit between the races and the desire for peaceful reform rather than violent revolution.

Another ground for hope was the contact made with the ANC by the Institute for a Democratic Alternative for South Africa (IDAS). Headed by the former Leader of the Progressive Federal Party (PFP) Dr van Zyl Slabbert, about sixty South Africans met

WHAT OF THE FUTURE?

in Zambia with executive members of the ANC and satisfied that organization that they were fully committed to non-racialism and equality. Reports from this meeting indicated that there were signs that the ANC was willing to compromise in any negotiated settlement. During this period hopeful signs were also emerging from Natal where the Indaba proposals were put forward. The Natal provincial council and the KwaZulu government launched a constitutional conference (Indaba) to formulate proposals for a legislative body for their regions. Natal is one of the country's four provinces and KwaZulu is the most populous black state and the plan was for a multi-racial entity with a majority rule balanced by certain guaranteed veto rights for minority groups. If the state would accept this proposal it could then be applied to other provinces. This showed, despite the somewhat lukewarm reception by the National Party, that black and white could work together and come up with positive suggestions for the future of the country. If greater guarantees for the rights of minorities were to be inserted into the plan the state might look with more favour on it. So far the state is willing to let KwaZulu and Natal share a common administration but not a legislature. Hence in 1987 legislation to create a joint executive authority was enacted and provision made for similar regional administration in the rest of the country.

On the bright side of the picture, too, South Africa's first three black ambassadors were appointed, the first black judge appeared in the Natal courts, schools closed in 1986 were reopened, spending on black education was increased by 40%, ninety million rand was given to upgrade the Alexandria township, job reservations for whites at the mines were repealed, more central business districts were opened for trading by all races, salary parity was achieved by black social workers, most cinemas and drive-ins were desegregated, the level of unrest diminished, and in 1988 the Sharpville Six were granted a stay of execution. The latter event resulted from the need to re-examine a witness but the whole affair excited world-wide comment and included pleas for mercy from many countries including Britain and the USA. The six faced execution after being convicted of the murder of a black town councillor but they were part of a mob estimated to be about a hundred and it had not been proven that they had 'contributed causally to the death of the deceased'. All that could be said was that they had shared the common purpose of the crowd that stoned and burnt to death Jacob Dlamini, deputy mayor of the town council, outside his Sharpville house on 3 September 1984.

The government itself made a move towards change with its confirmation that the plans for the National Statutory Council would proceed. The intention of this proposal is to create a new constitution for the country to satisfy the blacks, hence the need for negotiation with all leaders. It is proposed that cabinet ministers, including the chairmen of the various tricameral (three races) own affairs administrations, leaders of the self-governing states and leaders of urban black communities and interest groups sit on such a Council to plan jointly the future of the country. Commenting on this in parliament on 17 April 1986, Botha said: 'It offers us the opportunity of negotiating with each other our views and terms for a new South Africa instead of allowing preconditions to withhold us from meeting around the table.'

In 1987 government negotiators were canvassing the views of black leaders as to how black representatives might be identified and selected to take part and it was recognized that elections of them might take place. The Deputy Minister of Information, Dr Stoggel van der Merwe, was also appointed Deputy Minister of Constitutional Planning and given the special task of trying to get these representative black leaders to the conference table.

On 21 April 1988 Botha made an important policy statement in which he said he was prepared to consider a suggestion by a recently deceased black homeland leader that the Council should be renamed the 'Great Indaba' (Indaba is the Zulu word for conference) and he hinted that blacks could eventually be appointed to the cabinet. The government was working on draft legislation for new elected regional assemblies for blacks living outside the

WHAT OF THE FUTURE?

homelands. These would serve as a basis for their participation in a formal forum for deliberation.

Reluctantly we now turn away from these signs of hope and see the balance swinging in the other and more pessimistic direction. Black organizations such as the UDF rejected the National council proposals and P. W. Botha attacked meetings of business men, politicians, and churchmen with the ANC. The state banned the UDF and other black protest movements and virtually left the church as the only centre of demonstration for justice and basic rights. Unrest in the black townships was reduced to a minimum with strong security measures by police and army.

The ANC continued with its bombing campaign and exploded the biggest bomb yet detonated in the Republic at the South African Defence Force headquarters in Johannesburg. It injured sixty-eight people and brought the number to one hundred and twenty injured and twelve killed in the eleven bomb explosions from January to July 1987.

While these explosions which brought death and injury to many black civilians made people rethink their alliance to the ANC and caused some whites to commit themselves to what the Afrikaner called 'the chicken run', i.e. leaving the country, further trouble developed among the miners. Having adopted the Freedom Charter of the ANC, the National Union of Mines flexed its muscles on the 9 August 1987 by calling the biggest strike on South African mines in the history of the country: 250,000 miners struck for a 30% increase in wages. Memories of the miner's strike in Britain that toppled the Heath government encouraged the hope that such action might end apartheid and overthrow Pretoria.

This did prove a test for the government, worried about the growing power of the unions since they were legalized about ten years ago. Instead of the unions acting as it was hoped as escape valves for black discontent, they had become crucibles of black power. In the event it watched anxiously as trouble erupted between employer and employee which claimed the deaths of ten people, and sighed with relief that the miners failed in their political aim, though they did achieve a pay rise of over 20%. This brought them nearer to parity with white workers. But one weakness on the miners' part was exposed, the fact that over 100,000 blacks from Lesotho, 50,000 from Mozambique, and many from Malawi, Botswana, Swaziland are employed in the gold mines. These workers were unwilling to lose their jobs for South African political causes.

However, this movement towards socialism worried the business community dedicated to capitalist principles. Gavin Relly, chairman of Anglo-American, though he was involved in a meeting with the ANC, declared that the reforming process was the way forward, not revolution. He argued that the most successful economies in the world have a preference for the free enterprise system, a belief in less government rather than more, and base their reliance on the market in the management of the country. From this he contends flows deregulation, privatization and investment in education.

Botha's programme for an undivided South Africa with one citizenship, equality before the law, equal opportunity, and full participation by all in negotiated democratic institutions, is better than a Marxism which promises much but cannot deliver. He called upon the business section of the community to do more for its workers, and his corporation will lead the way by building homes for them on lands adjacent to the mining areas and encourage home ownership and the holding of shares in the company. In this connection he strongly opposed the Group Areas Act for how can industrialization take place without urbanization?

We have noted in previous chapters that this Act remains on the statute books[1] and has caused problems for many blacks wanting to live in white areas. The only concession given in 1987 was the decision of the President's Council to recommend a local option for official desegregation of certain 'grey' areas, but the Act should be retained. This was the final straw for the coloured chairman of the House of Representatives, the Revd H. J. Hendrickse who, after a number of quarrels with the Prime Minister, re-

WHAT OF THE FUTURE?

signed. However it does seem quite inconsistent to abolish the Mixed Marriages Act and allow people to marry across the colour line but to maintain laws on the statute book which prevent them being able to live together legally. Despite the right-wing Afrikaner opposition to the dissolving of this last barrier to unity it is difficult to see how the Nationalist party dedicated to reform can logically retain it if they want to be seen to be in earnest in what they are doing for change in the country.

The 1987 elections provided them with a setback as the right-wing Conservative party, whose manifesto stated that partition was the way and the whites must have their own land where only they would enjoy political rights, won 22 seats and became the official opposition in parliament. P. W. Botha fought the election on the platform to negotiate with all the country's leaders towards a new system of power-sharing intended to rule out the domination of one race over another and the maintaining of law and order while the reforming process continued. His party was returned with 123 seats. The result, a definite swing to the right, was greeted with despondency. Archbishop Desmond Tutu said that it heralded 'the darkest stage' in the country's history and Allan Boesak commented: 'The government has made the peaceful process of change impossible.' Political leaders agreed. The UDF declared that the stage had been set 'for the deepening of the conflict' and the Zulu leader, Chief Mangosuthu Buthelezi, usually optimistic, exclaimed that he was 'totally appalled' by the outcome.

Perhaps it was to satisfy this right-wing opposition that Botha moved to the banning of black opposition groups, but whatever the reason it has made the church the only continuing centre of black protest. It is therefore moving more strongly along the lines indicated in the last chapter, namely non-violent resistance. Thus the South African Council of Catholic Laity which represents 2.3 million catholics described Botha's government as 'morally illegitimate' and the Catholic church inserted advertisements in the newspapers accusing the state of 'serious abuses' of power in its denial of human rights and repression. This outspoken criticism was followed by an act of defiance by the Anglican church against the law prohibiting public protests about detention without trial. A 'service for detainees' was organized by Desmond Tutu in Capetown cathedral where the Archbishop warned the government: 'You are powerful, perhaps even very powerful, but you are not God.' Confrontation was only avoided by the state allowing that prayers for the release of detainees were not prohibited during a religious service. Indeed the state hesitated to move against Tutu because of his great following in the Republic, and left him alone despite his outspoken criticism of its policies during his visit to Britain and other countries in 1988.

The successor to the Revd Beyers Naude as general secretary of the South African Council of Churches, the Revd Frank Chicane, who was in Britain at the same time as Tutu, sees clearly the suffering involved in such resistance. In an open letter to 'all those who care' he wrote:

> No one really wants to go to the cross, or the way of the cross, but it has dawned on me in a new way that it does not look like we can achieve our liberation in South Africa without going through the cross . . . It looks like it is in our death that we shall rise again into a new and just society . . . It looks like that it is through this seemingly hopeless situation that there can be hope even to free or liberate the oppressors and those who are intoxicated with power . . . It did not occur to me that I will be required to go the whole way through . . . Yes I am scared about this reality, I wish I could avoid it . . . so that I can also live a normal life like other people. I am scared that if this is the will of the Lord I will not escape it . . . I am now halfway through to Jerusalem . . .[2]

Some debate ensued in 1988, however, concerning the position of the Anglican church when it was said that it had accepted the controversial 'Lusaka document' which recognized that liberation movements are compelled to use force. But this was denied by the

WHAT OF THE FUTURE?

Anglican Bishop of Johannesburg, Duncan Buchanan, who said that such reports were untrue and that the Anglican church did not endorse violence but understood how violence begets violence.

On 29 February Tutu and Boesak attempted to lead a march of 150 clergymen of all denominations to Parliament to present a petition against the curbs placed on the activities of political organizations. Both of them accept that this pathway of non-violent resistance will have serious consequences for them. Boesak, addressing his congregation at Belville in the western Cape on the 27 March 1988, used words reminiscent of Chicane: 'If I die it will be because of the faithfulness to the gospel of Jesus Christ that I have tried my best to fulfil ...' Both he and Tutu continue to receive death threats and the march of 29 February brought strong criticism from the state and the DRC.

Botha's position on the relation of church and state is clear from what we said in previous chapters and he warned church members not to be taken 'in tow by a few radical clergy and certain academics who are attempting to force liberation theology on the churches from above ...' and he warned that the church was being turned into a 'battleground against the government'. When Tutu went to see Botha to plead for the Sharpville Six he was harangued by him for his liberation theology: 'Are you acting on behalf of the kingdom of God or the kingdom promised by the ANC and the South African Communist party? If it is the latter say so but do not hide behind the structures and cloth of the Christian church because Christianity and Marxism are irreconcilable opposites.'

From the DRC came the criticism that such demonstrations were seeking confrontation not reconciliation and led to the cancellation of an arranged historic meeting of the NGK with the Anglican church and the SACC. Commentators on this saw the DRC taking the side of the state rather than the church at large in South Africa. I do not think that this is a proper interpretation. The DRC is united with all the other churches against apartheid and has a crucial role to play. It has been called the 'National party at prayer' (in the last white parliament 70% of the representatives and 80% of the cabinet were members) and it has confessed that it was wrong in its attitude to the system and would do all in its power to change it. The present moderator of the General Synod, Professor John Heyns, has said that the church must fulfil its prophetic function and oppose a state that continues apartheid and has called on all churches for 'critical solidarity' in this matter. As H. W. Turner comments: 'The DRC holds the key to much of the change required in South Africa. At last it seems to have inserted the key in the lock. It may grate a bit, and even jam for a while, but it seems to have begun to turn.'[3] And, he further notes, that the fact that 1,500 conservatives seceded in recent times shows that they know that the DRC means business.

What seems to be the difference between the other churches and the DRC is the method of bringing about change. The DRC has the powerful task of influencing the government directly by discussion and verbal protest concerning injustice. It cannot restrict itself to the 'spiritual' as Botha thinks a church should, but must become involved in persuading the state to hasten its social change. The other churches, however, are using a different method which does involve confrontation and is much more dangerous for themselves, namely non-violent resistance. Both parties should respect the method of each other keeping before them the same goal: the complete dismantling of apartheid. United in this purpose they have a vital role in bringing about change.

Certainly the church in Britain rallied to the support of Tutu and Dr Runcie sent the Rt Revd Keith Sutton on a mission to the country to assure them of this. The bishops of the Anglican church in South Africa also expressed their solidarity with their Archbishop and declared that they were prepared to accept that the church was now 'under siege.' Catholics too, as we have noted, condemned the behaviour of the state despite the fact that Pretoria moved to the banning for three months of one of their influential newspapers.

WHAT OF THE FUTURE?

Another gloomy aspect of life in the Republic is the tension which has developed between black and black. We have seen this in the black townships and the case of the Sharpville Six is a reminder of how blacks deal with their so called traitors; councillors who they see as co-operating with the state. But even more serious was the murderous rivalry which manifested itself between the UDF and Inkatha in townships around Maritzburg in 1987. In two months 200 people had been killed and the Inkatha president Mangosuthu Buthelezi posed the question: 'How in God's name can I be forgiving and how can I be forgetful?' A UDF spokesman was equally unforgiving: 'Comrades will never agree or accept peace talks if there are still Inkatha people with blood on their hands.'[4]

It is difficult to understand the root cause of the trouble. Some see it in the forceful way Inkatha tries to recruit new members by press-gang methods, others think it is due to the continuing struggle for supremacy between the two organizations. The conflict goes back to 1983 when the UDF was attacked by Buthelezi for attempting to create 'no go' areas in his own backyard. In 1987 both organizations used methods of killing which were particularly harrowing and included stabbing and hacking to death. The black editor of the Soweto newspaper wrote: 'If this is the type of retribution which will become common when blacks rule blacks then perhaps we need a great deal more oppression to make us humble, responsible and dignified in our anger against oppression.' Winnie Mandela, however, offered to act as a mediator between the rival groups and this was welcomed by Buthelezi.[5]

Conflict too was evident between white and white, though this was usually confined to a war of words. We have noted earlier that the Conservative party headed by Dr Andries Treurnicht won 22 seats in the 1987 whites only election and since then they have been striving to increase their seats in the general election which will be held in 1990. Signs are that they might well do this if recent by-elections are an indicator. In Randfontein, west of Johannesburg, they defeated the National party candidate in

March 1988 and this meant that they had won three by-elections in the space of a month. Thus they showed their ability not only to do well in the rural Transvaal but in middle-class urban areas, for Randfontein's voters fear black advancement. This is one of the reasons given for what has been called the 'white backlash' in response to the reforming policy of the National party, but there are other factors such as the depressed economy, the freeze on public sector wages, the government plan to privatize state enterprises that were originally set up to provide protected employment for Afrikaners, and the basic uncertainty of voters as to where the country is heading.[6]

How real is this threat? In the 1987 elections Botha's party did reasonably well, increasing its representation in parliament from 118 to 123 seats whereas the Conservatives won only 22 (13.3%) of the 166 directly elected seats. The remainder went to the PFP and smaller parties, but the Conservatives won 26% of the vote and if it could continue nationally its Randfontein success in the forthcoming general election it would increase dramatically its parliamentary seats. Transvaal is very important here since it has the largest share of the white population and parliamentary seats and of the 123 seats won by the government in 1987, 47 are in Transvaal and 14 in the Orange Free State. Botha believes that he can hold on to the English-speaking vote which welcomes his reforms but this is a more fickle vote and if his reforms are not accelerated the votes could move back to the PFP.

In conclusion, some comments on the two ways of bringing about change in South Africa which we have noted throughout this book: revolution and reform. Revolution was embraced by Mr Oliver Tambo of the ANC in a TV interview in 1988 on the ground that this was just but its revolutionary method of bombing supermarkets and killing civilians is not in line with the just war concept that insists that non-combatants, neutrals and third parties must not be harmed. Also the last resort is a criterion for embarking upon such a conflict and we do not think that this

WHAT OF THE FUTURE?

situation has been reached in the Republic. Only when negotiations have taken place and failed can this be argued.

Moreover, the goal of the revolution as laid down in the ANC Freedom Charter is the happiness and prosperity of the people. But, after a bloody conflict, what are they going to inherit: a broken-down economy, shattered industries and cities, thousands of dead and wounded. The picture is too appalling to contemplate. This way of revolution will not lead to raising the living standards of blacks but depress them for years to come. And is the West ready to have another Third World country on its hands? Again, we are simply thinking of what would occur in an open conflict between black and white, and not daring to consider a possible black civil war between Zulus and the ANC as an aftermath. But, as we have seen, the killing between the blacks of the ANC/UDF in Natal and the followers of Buthelezi augurs ill for a future dispensation based on the ways of men of violence. As Paul Lehman said '... revolutions regularly eat their own children, and they do so because, held captive by the idolatrous self-imaging of their own ideology, they cannot avoid new oppressions ...'[7]

The best way forward, then, would be by the reforming process but what we have currently in the Republic is repressive reform. The state of emergency, though necessary to prevent the breakdown of law and order, has also hardened the attitudes of blacks whom the process of reform is supposed to help. This is certainly not a peaceful way to the negotiating table. Indeed the question needs to be faced: How can reform really get off the ground while black leaders who should now be part of the negotiating team are in detention? Unrest has declined in the country, so there is little reason for not releasing all detainees and since the renunciation of violence is not now a precondition for release surely it is time for Nelson Mandela to be set free. Mandela has become such a cult figure that his release would have the effect of helping the world to believe that Botha's reforms were really in earnest. But the current hard censorship, the banning of black political organizations, and the presence of military and police in the townships, only serve to make the world believe that this reform is simply a patching up of the system or the moving of chairs around a room which remains the same.

There is some justification for this criticism, for it could be argued that so far such reform continues to operate in an apartheid framework and could be seen as reinforcing segregation. This can be illustrated in various ways. If we look at the new constitutional dispensation introduced in September 1985 and take education as an example we note that under the tricameral parliament there are five ministries concerned with this area. Each racial group has a different ministry and education is treated as an 'own-affair' of each group. Such segregation is opposed not only by the blacks but from the economic viewpoint the duplication of scarce resources and facilities is a most costly way of achieving equal education for all. Obviously the state wants to keep talking about 'your own affairs' to the different race groups rather than 'our affairs' which would have a more majority decision or rule about it.

Then there are the following incidents that make the world think that Botha is not serious in his reforming zeal. The white minister of education and culture said that government schools were an 'own affair' and could not be open to blacks. The Indian minister of affairs stressed that certain conditions would have to be met before blacks could go to Indian schools. A Pretoria high school refused to allow a black athlete from Natal to run on its track and the navy said that coloured instructors could not train white recruits. Black medical students were barred from certain women's wards at the Johannesburg hospital and in a rural town a black teacher was barred from the public library because the white council said that its library was its 'own affair'.

The fact is that racial thinking about 'own affairs' has so dominated South African society over the years that it is very difficult to think on other lines. I am glad to say that such petty apartheid is slowly breaking down but a framework of reform that emphasized unity rather than diversity would go a long way to make for

WHAT OF THE FUTURE?

better relations between the races. Some black revolutionary organizations need to take this to heart as well for they contend that blacks alone can bring about change and do not need the whites or other races. Fortunately both the ANC and UDF generally take the opposite view as their statements and the non-racial composition of the UDF indicate.

Assuming then that negotiations will have to take place, how is the conflict to be resolved between the ANC who want majority rule and the whites who see this as a total loss of power? Here the West sides with the blacks and wishes to project its democratic way of government into the African continent. But democracy has not had a good history on the African continent for it is estimated that fifteen countries have had one coup since independence, fifteen others have had two or more, and by 1983 fifty governments had been overthrown in independent Africa and thirty of Africa's countries had experienced a *coup d'état*. Reasons are tribal diversity and enmity, shaky economics, and land claims. Dissidents have been killed, detained or exiled in a South African manner, as the parliamentary democracy imposed by colonial powers broke down and the dictators emerged. It is so easy, as Plato noted, for this to happen.

Democracy at its best of course is the right way and has always appealed to British philosophers such as John Locke (1632–1704) and John Stuart Mill (1773–1836). Locke was very influential in the framing of the American Declaration of Independence and the constitution but Locke did not see clearly, as Mill did, the tyranny often exercised by the majority. Minorities need protection and representation so that some form of consensus might be reached in decision making. Since this has not happened in other parts of Africa the whites in the Republic fear what would happen to them under a black majority government. Steps would need to be taken to guarantee such rights even if an outside force such as Britain or the United Nations had to act as guarantor to ensure that in a future settlement it was being carried out. But there is another problem here: the ANC charter is communistic which could lead to the taking of property from the whites and giving it to the dispossessed. This is not Western-style democracy which makes room for capitalism, so concessions would need to be made in any negotiations about this crucial matter.

Again, democracy as laid down by J. S. Mill was for a mature and informed society, but the majority in the Republic have not had the benefit of proper education and it is only in recent times that black education is showing signs of improvement. Hence blacks are unable to understand and criticize politicians who want votes and power and could be manipulated 'intimidation has often been rife in other parts of Africa) so that corrupt individuals could get into government. This in itself points to the need for a period of time before majority rule could take place in the country.

Various astute and experienced politicians on the South African scene who have contended for the end of apartheid over the years see a federal structure as one of the best solutions to this perplexing problem. One such is Helen Suzman, traditional opponent of apartheid, nominated twice for the Nobel Prize, and honoured by both Oxford and Harvard universities with doctorates. She is now sixty-nine years of age having entered parliament in 1953 and despite threats to her life has maintained an opposition to apartheid which is most impressive. In 1986 she castigated the government for its state of emergency, condemned it for its detention policy and accused the police of torturing black youths in prison. From 1961 to 1974 she stood alone in parliament as the sole member of the PFP and in 1986 she visited Nelson Mandela and emerged saying that she did not believe that he was a Communist and that he was the key to solving the problems of the country. She contends that whites isolate themselves from the suffering and poverty of the blacks and points out that many have not even been to a black township. Opposing sanctions which she believes will damage the economy and mean more unemployment for blacks, she favours a federal system for the country which would be decided not on racial grounds but geographic. Areas would have their own administration while such matters as defence and international trade would be in the hands of the central federal government. Elections would be by proportional representation and a bill of rights would protect minorities. The country including the homelands would consist of multi-racial states.

This would involve some form of power-sharing with all races having a part in the government of the country and such a proposal is most likely to enter into future negotiations. A peaceful way to it needs to be found and the conditions created with the release of political prisoners whom the people regard as their leaders. The ANC, despite its revolutionary stand and attitude of confrontation, has said that it does not wish to inherit a third world country which could be the result of continued warfare and increased sanctions by the external world. And, it knows that it needs the expertise of the whites to help run the country.

Suzman is trying to move away from the ethnic or group factor since it tends to make racial thinking about their own affairs dominant. Others, however, consider that it is more realistic to recognize that this will continue to exist and in a federal structure each group must be fully represented.

However, whatever form of structure evolves and the main urgency at the moment is to get negotiations started, there must be eventually a move towards majority rule. In the long term it is not possible for any minority group by use of a veto to block the will of the majority though it will take considerable time for a powerful minority group like the whites to accept this.

This brings us back again to the question of the protection of minorities and how far the whites can be reassured that a bill of rights will give them sufficient protection. Certainly it is not too optimistic to predict a South Africa with a black president and a majority of blacks in the top echelons of government and a white minority providing the technical know-how and expertise.[8] What the time-scale for this would be is most difficult to predict and largely depends on the speed of successful negotiations. This will call for flexibility on the part of black organizations like the ANC and the hope that the right-wing Conservative white party will not increase their growth. If the latter were to succeed it would set the clock back for years to come.[9]

Here the church can play a crucial role not only acting as a centre of protest in a non-violent way but trying to be a mediator between black and white. The other churches it is hoped will see the importance of the DRC in this since so many of the National Party belong to it and the DRC should endeavour to become more and more united with them in their common purpose. Further division over methods of doing this need to be played down otherwise the church as a whole will have missed a great opportunity of leading a united drive towards a new dispensation for the country.

A final thought. Sometimes when travelling through this beautiful country I have been so overwhelmed by the loveliness of the landscape or the marvellous feats of human engineering that I have got out of the car and simply stared at it all. How is it, I have thought, that in a country of such promise people can behave so badly to one another? Is it because of economics or racial prejudice or simply sin . . . Surely a country like this with a people of great skill and determination can find a way out of the present impasse and create a just society where all can share in the good things which it offers. Of course it will take patience, the sharing of power, the forgetting of past wrongs, and the willingness to work together on the part of all races . . . but that the 'beloved country' can do it, I am sure.

Appendix

Checklist of Parties and Organizations

African National Congress (ANC). Emerged out of the African native congress founded in 1912. Objective: to end racial discrimination and obtain franchise for blacks. It is non-racial, stresses class as well as race in the struggle and advocates co-operation with all races. Originally non-violent it eventually became involved in attacks on government targets. Most of the leaders, including Nelson Mandela, were sentenced in 1964 to life imprisonment. The current leader who is in exile is Oliver Tambo. In 1928 Moscow recognized it as the representative of the oppressed masses of South Africa and by 1974 members of the South African Communist Party were part of the leadership. Headquarters: Lusaka, Zambia, with offices in London and other countries. In 1983 at the East German celebration of the centenary of Karl Marx the ANC declared its 'natural alliance with the Soviet Union and the world socialist system as a whole'. On the other hand it has stated that it is by no means the puppet of Moscow. It was banned in 1961.

Afrikan Weerstandsbeweging (AWB). The Afrikan resistance movement established in 1973 at Heidelberg. Current president: Eugene Terre Blanche. Aim is to ensure the continued existence of the Afrikaner-Boer nation which it insists is in accord with the Bible, the Protestant faith, and the Oath taken at Blood River where the Boers defeated the Zulus (1838). Their intention is to create a Boer National Republic separate from the Republic of

South Africa with its own government and a stress on white origins and racial purity.

Azanian People's Organization (AZAPO). Formed in 1979 as a successor to the Black Consciousness movement. It stresses black identity, pride and respect. The membership excludes whites.

Black Consciousness movement (BC). Centred upon an awareness of the black situation and identity which developed in the seventies under the leadership of Steve Biko who was founder of the SA student's organization and honorary president of the Black people's convention. It is associated with the Soweto uprising of 1976. Biko died in detention 1977. The movement was subsequently banned.

Conservative Party (CP). Founded in 1982 by A. P. Treunicht as a reaction to the policies of reform being carried through by the state. Same aim as the AWB i.e. a policy of partition with whites having their own land where only they would enjoy political rights. It is not prepared to negotiate the future of whites with any other group of whatever colour and claims that the only solution is for each ethnic group to govern itself.

Congress of SA Trade Unions (COSATU). Formed in 1985 with 34 affiliates and a membership of half a million. It has accepted the Freedom Charter of the ANC.

Frente Nacional de Libertacao de Angola (FNLA). Formed in 1962 and is an armed opposition group in Angola with about 14,000 adherents. Somewhat dormant in recent years but showing signs of revival. It opposes the government of Jose Eduardo dos Santos which gained control of the country in 1976. FNLA does not co-operate with the other liberation movement, UNITA.

Herstigte Nasionale Party (HNP). Reconstituted national party created in 1969 as a consequence of friction in the National Party between the traditionalists and the revisionists. Currently it is in reaction to the state's reforms stressing on the one hand the

APPENDIX

wrongs done to the Afrikaner by the British and the blacks in the past, and on the other that the blacks are a simple people and not yet ready for a multi-racial society. It says that when it comes to power it will negotiate with the blacks on the basis of separate development and the partition of the country. The Conservative Party and the HNP have tried to form an alliance but without success so far.

Homelands. Sometimes called national states or bantustans for blacks. Some are independent of the RSA others are self-governing within it. They consist of Transkei, Bophuthatswana, Venda, Ciskei (independent) and Gazankulu, Kangwane, Kwandebele, KwaZulu, Lebowa, QwaQwa (self-governing).

Institute for a Democratic Alternative for South Africa (INDASA). A recent multi-racial grouping dedicated to achieving a non-racial and democratic country. It is not a political party but an organization which seeks to make community contact with all who oppose apartheid and are seeking to remove the distrust that is evident among the races. Conferences, research, and the gathering of unbiased information are part of its programme and representatives met with the ANC in Dakar, Senegal and issued a joint statement on the desirability of a non-racial democracy. The leader is Dr Van Zyl Slabbert formerly head of the Progressive Federal Party.

INKATHA. Re-established in 1975 by the current president Gatsha Buthelezi with a membership of two million. It is multi-racial but almost entirely composed of Zulus. The youth brigade together with its trade movement (UWUSA) was involved recently in violence with the ANC. Objectives are: abolishing all forms of discrimination, creating equal opportunities for all, encouraging patriotism and national unity and co-operating locally and internationally with all political parties for the attainment of African unity. Partnership with the state in attaining these objectives is not unacceptable and the organization has in recent times produced the KwaZulu Indaba (conference) proposals for a regional political settlement. The plan would mean that KwaZulu and Natal would be governed as a multi-racial entity with majority rule balanced by certain guaranteed veto rights for minority groups.

Mozambique National Resistance (MNR) or Renamo. The rebel group which has been causing so many problems for the government there. These guerrilla fighters were originally set up by the Rhodesian army to counter Mugabe's forces. It is generally recognized that they have the support of Pretoria.

National Party (NP). Founded in 1914 and won general election in 1948. Instituted apartheid on the grand design of Dr H. F. Verwoerd who was assassinated in 1966. He was succeeded as Prime Minister by B. J. Vorster who resigned in 1978. P. W. Botha was leader until early 1989, when he was succeeded by F. W. Klerk, and was accused by the right wingers of splitting the Afrikaners by the new constitution (1984) which included coloured and Indians in parliament. Dissident MPs formed new Conservative Party in 1982. The party continues in power with its victory in the 1987 election.

New Republic Party (NRP). Started in recent times by Wynand Maland and Denis Worrall, formerly SA's ambassador to London, as a breakaway from the National Party but did not do well in the 1987 elections. It believes that blacks should be in parliament as soon as possible as a interim measure to create a proper climate for negotiating a long-term solution. Supported the Natal Indaba and tries to get such negotiations at a national level.

Pan African Congress (PAC). Formed in 1959 with the stress on Africa for blacks only. Europeans and Asians cannot belong to the Congress. It was a reaction too to the feeling among many blacks that the ANC had been taken over by the white dominated SA Communist Party for its own ideological ends. It was banned in 1961.

APPENDIX

Progressive Federal Party (PFP). Formed on 5 September 1977 and on the 30 November won 17 seats in the election to parliament and became the official opposition. Refused to co-operate in the President's Council of the new constitution (1984). In 1979 Dr F. Van Zyl Slabbert, a former professor of sociology at Stellenbosch University, had been elected leader and in the election of 1981 the PFP won 26 seats. Slabbert resigned in 1986. Its main aims are a regional federal system of government, the removing of discrimination on grounds of colour, a single citizenship for all South Africans regardless of ethnic origin, the protection of individual and minority rights, a bill of rights, and the convening of a national convention in which representatives of all population groups will participate. The party lost its status as the official opposition to the Conservative Party in the elections of 1987. It rejects majority rule.

South West Africa People's Organization (SWAPO). The guerrilla movement which fought for the independence of Namibia. It is sometimes called PLAN (People's Liberation Army of Namibia).

United Democratic Front (UDF). Formed in 1983 with 575 affiliates. Its objective is to unite all anti-apartheid organizations. Accused of being the political front for the ANC, it has the support of such church leaders as Desmond Tutu and Allan Boesak. It has played a major part in articulating black grievances and in 1987 formed the South African Youth Congress (SAYCO) and the Women's Congress. So far has vetoed the state's initiatives for change.

Uniao Nacional Para Independencia Total de Angola (UNITA). Created in 1966 as an independent insurgent movement to free Angola from Portuguese control but involved in conflict with other movements such as the FNLA. Led by Dr Jonas Savimibi it claims upwards of 75,000 armed followers and the support of 60% of Angolans. Objectives: to achieve a democratic form of government in the country with the protection of minority rights, freedom of the press, private enterprise, the development of the economy (SA plays a large role here and this is recognized), and establishment of good relations both locally and internationally. It says that it wants dialogue with the present government of Angola to achieve a national unity and the withdrawal of the Cuban troops from the country. Despite the recent arrangement for a Cuban withdrawal, UNITA intends to topple the present government if agreement with it cannot be reached.

Notes

Chapter One   Arrival

1. The secretary of the SACC before Desmond Tutu was Mr Joh Rees who was charged with misappropriating 275,000 rand of the council's money. He was convicted on twenty-nine counts, but the SACC survived the scandal.
2. H. V. Morton, *In Search of South Africa*, Methuen 1948. I am indebted to this author for his impressive descriptions of the country.
3. The post is now held by Mr Adrian Vlok.

Chapter Two   The Mother City

1. It was desegregated in 1989.
2. John DeGruchy, *Bonhoeffer and South Africa*, Eerdmans, Grand Rapids 1984, p. 13.
3. For a more detailed account of the Institute and Naudé see R. J. Neuhaus, *Dispensations*, Eerdmans, Grand Rapids 1986, pp. 99f.
4. Since my visit a new town has been developed for the people of Crossroads and the State has abolished influx control.
5. In 1989 Botha resigned the leadership of the National Party because of illness, but retained the Presidency of the State. Mr F. W. Klerk became the new leader.
6. Mandela has now been moved from a Capetown clinic to a house in the grounds of a Paarl prison.

Chapter Four   A State of Emergency

Reports from both local and international newspapers and the South African Foundation have been very useful in the compiling of this chapter and I would acknowledge my debt.

Chapter Six   The Role of the Church

1. David J. Bosch, 'Afrikaner Civil Religion and Current South African Crisis', *The Princeton Seminary Bulletin*, vol. vii, no. 1, 1986, pp. 7ff.

NOTES

2. Ibid., p. 11.
3. I. J. Mosala and B. Tlhagale (eds), *The Unquestionable Right to be Free: Essays in Black Theology*, Skotaville Publishers, Johannesburg and Orbis Books, Maryknoll 1986.
4. Ibid., pp. 59ff.
5. S. Maimela in Ibid., pp. 108f.
6. T. Mofokeng in Ibid., pp. 114f.
7. B. Tlhagale in Ibid., pp. 136f.
8. Ibid., pp. 177ff.
9. *Saga of God Incarnate*, 2nd edn UNISA and T. & T. Clark 1988, Ch. 8.

Chapter Seven Violence or Non-Violence?

1. We are not discussing S. G. F. Brandon's thesis that Jesus was a rebel, for the Kairos document does not make use of it. See Brandon's *The Fall of Jerusalem and the Christian Church*, SPCK 1951, [2]1957, and *Jesus and the Zealots*, Manchester University Press 1967. Cf. Alan Richardson's critique, *The Political Christ*, SCM Press 1973, pp. 53ff.
2. C. E. B. Cranfield, 'The Christian's Political Responsibility according to the New Testament', *SJT* Vol. 15 No. 2 June 1962, p. 183. A recent book by John Helgeland, Robert J. Daley and J. Patout Burns, *Christians and the Military*, SCM Press 1987, is however against the pacifist position.
3. See *Table Talk*, *SJT* Occasional Papers No. 10, 1963, p. 76. For a full discussion see *Church Dogmatics*, 111/4, S55,2, and *The Knowledge of God and the Service of God*, London 1938, pp. 229-32.
4. Ibid., p. 76.
5. Ibid., p. 81.
6. Peter Bishop, *A Technique for Loving*, SCM Press 1981, p. 99.
7. Kenneth Kaunda, *Kaunda on Violence*, ed. C. Morris, Collins 1980, p. 57.
8. Peter Bishop, op cit., p. 99.
9. Ibid., p. 85.
10. See my *Loyal to King Billy*, Hurst 1987.
11. Peter Bishop, op. cit., p. 120.
12. Ibid., p. 123. The Pope on his recent visit to Southern Africa denounced both apartheid and the use of violence to end it. He called for a negotiated peace.

Chapter Eight What of the Future?

1. The Group Areas Act and the Registration Act, which classifies all South Africans in racial categories, are the last bastion of apartheid.

NOTES

2. Frank Chicane, 'I am halfway to Jerusalem', *Reform*, September 1987, p. 11.

3. H. W. Turner, 'The Afrikaner and critical solidarity', *Herald*, March 1988, p. 17. However, the Revd Dr Nicol Smith disagrees that the DRC has abandoned apartheid and proof of this, he says, lies in the fact that at the Synod of 1987 separate churches for different racial groups are still justified. *Herald*, May 1988, p. 13.

4. Patrick Laurence, 'Black politics – 1987', *South Africa Foundation Review*, Johannesburg, vol. 14, no. 1, January 1988, p. 2.

5. In 1989, Winnie Mandela herself got into trouble with anti-apartheid organizations and the police over the accusation that her bodyguard had been involved in the murder of a fourteen-year-old black boy.

6. Michael Hornsby, 'Far right stakes a claim to power', *The Times*, 31 March 1988, p. 10.

7. Quoted by A. J. MaKelway, 'Perichoretic possibilities in Barth's doctrine of male and female', *Princeton Seminary Bulletin*, vol. vii, no. 3, p. 143.

8. Kurt von Schirnding, 'SA in the year 2000', *South Africa Foundation Review*, Johannesburg, vol. 14, no. 1, January 1988, p. 8.

9. Another general election could take place in 1989 and the municipal elections of October 1988 showed that the Conservative Party continue to gain ground, though there was no watershed swing away from the National Party. These councils are designed by the State as a building block for a new constitution in which all races would participate. But there was a black election boycott (only 20% voted) and showed that there continued to be 'a widespread political alienation among metropolitan blacks', i.e. only 12% vote in Soweto (*South African Foundation Review*, Johannesburg, December 1988, Vol. 14, No. 12, pp. 2f.).

Index

African National Congress, 4, 13f., 56ff., 59, 63, 79, 81, 87, 90f., 92, 98, 102f., 105, 121, 127, 139f., 147, 149, 151, 158f., 161ff., 167
Afrikaner, 8ff., 98f., 101f., 114f.
Afrikan Weerstandsbeweging, 167f.
Anglican Church, 31f., 154, 156
Armed rebellion, 138
Azanian People's Organization, 72f., 119, 168

Banning order, 28
Battle of Blood River, 9
Biko, S., 3ff., 119
Black Consciousness, 63, 71, 73, 118, 168
Black theology, 118ff.
Boer War, 9, 12
Boesak, A., 34f., 74f., 118, 148, 153, 155
Botha, P. W., 38, 56, 72, 80ff., 90f., 92ff., 128, 147f., 151ff., 155ff.
British settlers, 45f., 50f.
Buthelezi, M. G., 6, 56f., 60ff., 74, 80, 96, 106ff., 153, 157

Calvin, J., 113
Capitalism, 62f., 73
Catholic Church, 62f., 115, 153f., 156
Chicane, F., 154
Civil disobedience, 31, 35, 118
Collaborators, 73

Concentration camps, 99
Conscientious objection, 6, 26, 128, 138
Conscription, 101
Conservative Party, 38, 97, 153, 157f., 168
Crossroads, 33f., 100

Diaz, B., 19
Durham, Bishop of, 129
Dutch Reformed Church, 6, 15, 23, 155f.

Eminent Persons Group, 81

Front Line States, 77, 82
Frente Nacional de Libertacao de Angola, 77, 168

Gandhi, M., 142f.
Grahamstown, 45
Group Areas Act, 38, 67f., 89, 152f.
Guguletu, 20f.

Hendrickse, H. J., 152
Herstigte, Nasionale, 75f., 168
Heyns, J., 156
Hitler, A., 128f.
Homelands, 44f., 55ff., 169
Howe, G., 96, 112
Huddleston, T., 4, 61
Hurley, D., 62ff.

INDEX

Indaba, 149, 150
Indians, 36f., 58, 113
Inkatha, 57, 60, 107, 157, 169
Institute for a Democratic Alternative for South Africa, 148, 169

Just war, 131ff.

Kairos document, 115ff.
Kaunda, K., 142, 145f.
Kennedy, E., 72f., 85
King, M. L., 35, 121, 142f.
Kinnock, N., 85
Kruger, P., 11f.
Kruger Park, 64ff.
Kuyper, A., 114

Langa, 21
Locke, J., 161f.

Mandela, N., 14, 40, 71f., 73, 96, 107, 148, 162
Mandela, W., 71, 148, 157
Marx, K., 124, 125f.
Marxism, 30, 71, 118f., 124, 126, 129
Mill, J. S., 161f.
Mixed Marriage and Immorality Act, 95, 153
Moulder, J., 27
Mozambique National Resistance, 78f., 170

National Council, 107, 150
National Monument, 49ff.
National Party, 38, 170
Naude, B., 25, 36
New Constitution, 37f.
New Republic Party, 170
Nkomati Accord, 78, 80, 82
Nyanga, 20

Obedience to the State, 132ff., 136ff.
Origin of the coloured people, 19f.

Pacifism, 6, 131
Pan African Congress, 63, 105, 170
Pass laws, 94f.
Plato, 161
President's Council, 37
Progressive Federal Party, 38, 44, 158, 171

Relly, G., 152
Rhodes, C., 11, 26
Rhodes University, 45f., 49, 107, 110f.
Riebeeck, Jan van, 22, 30
Robben Island, 40
Russell, D., 34

Sanctions, 4, 80f., 82, 83f., 85f., 96, 103, 108
Sharpville, 14, 21, 26, 148
Sharpville Six, 149, 155, 157
South African Council of Churches, 4ff.
South West Africa People's Organization, 77f., 82, 171
Soweto, 2ff., 89, 96, 104, 148
State of emergency, 69ff.
Stellenbosch, 35
Suffering of Jesus and his followers, 132f.
Suzman, H., 45, 162

Tambo, O., 13, 72, 76, 85, 103ff., 147f., 158
Thatcher, M., 61, 82
Trade Union Movement, 70ff., 151ff., 168
Treurnicht, A. P., 10, 72, 75, 187
Turner, H. W., 156

INDEX

Tutu, Archbishop Desmond, 4ff., 73f., 148, 153, 155

United Democratic Front, 57, 60f., 71ff., 93, 105, 119, 157, 161, 171
Uitenhage riots, 43
Uniao Nacional Para Independencia Total de Angola, 77, 171
University of Bloemfontein, 98
University of Lesotho, 108f.
University of Natal, 98
University of the North, 66ff.
University of South Africa, 14ff.
University of Stellenbosch, 36
University of the Western Cape, 34
University of Witwatersrand, 27, 98
University of Zululand, 107f.

Verwoerd, H. F., 56f., 91, 98, 114f.
Violence and Christianity, 117f., 121ff., 131ff.
Voortrekker Monument, 7ff.

World Council of Churches, 5, 25

Xhosa, 46, 48, 93, 107

Zulus, 8f., 59f., 93, 106, 107f.